A Guide To
Bird Finding
In Vermont

by **Walter G. Ellison**

illustrations and maps by **Nancy L. Martin**

VERMONT INSTITUTE OF NATURAL SCIENCE
WOODSTOCK, VERMONT

1983

DEDICATION

This book is dedicated to my grandfather, Donald A. Sprout, a gentle man who I sincerely wish I might have known, and to my parents, George and Nancy Ellison, whose love of nature has guided me always.

© Copyright 1981
by the **VERMONT INSTITUTE OF NATURAL SCIENCE**
Except for brief passages quoted in a review, no part of this book (text, illustrations, or maps) may be reproduced without the written permission of the Vermont Institute of Natural Science.

Printed by:
Marus Printing Company
Hartland, Vermont 05048

FOREWORD

At last there is a bird finding guide for Vermont! Walter G. Ellison is a very appropriate person to write this guide, being one of Vermont's leading field birders, and a person who has been exploring Vermont's best birding areas for most of his twenty-six years. Walter, a University of Vermont graduate, has been Seasonal Editor of the Records of Vermont Birds since 1974, a summer field researcher on the Atlas Breeding Bird Project for six years, and a frequent leader of birding field trips. Walter's nickname to fellow birders is "The Ross's Gull", in memory of the winter day in Newburyport, Massachusetts when he was the first to identify the rare visitor.

The popularity of Walter's workshop on Vermont Bird Finding at the Annual Vermont Bird Conference convinced me that he should write, and VINS should publish, a book on this subject. VINS publishes this volume for all amateur naturalists with an interest in Vermont to enjoy! We express our thanks to the Fund for Preservation of Wildlife and Natural Areas for providing a loan from their revolving fund for publication, and thus making this book possible now.

Sarah B. Laughlin

Director, Vermont Institute of
Natural Science
December 1981

ACKNOWLEDGEMENTS

At an April hawk watch in 1977 a fellow birder commenting on the scarcity of information on birds for Vermont prompted me to state, somewhat rashly, that I was considering a work on birding areas for Vermont. Four years later the fruit of that offhand comment has ripened into this book. I can only hope that those who use this guide will derive as much pleasure from the areas it describes as I have in 're-searching' the accounts in these pages. It would be impossible to enumerate all those who have contributed to the final form of this book, but thanks are in order for those who have been most important. First, there would be no such thing as a bird finding guide were it not for Dr. Olin S. Pettingill; his books on bird finding have been a standard of excellence for thirty years. Secondly, I would like to offer heart-felt thanks to the regional experts who guided me to these areas and offered comments on the rough manuscript. These include: Don Clark, Barbara and Oliver Eastman, Eleanor Ellis, Bea Guyette, Larry Metcalf, Marion Metcalf, William J. Norse, Frank Oatman, Bruce Peterson, Roy Pilcher, Alan Pistorius and Wayne Scott. Doug Kibbe made many help-ful editorial suggestions on the text. Robert G. Brown was of in-valuable service in the indexing of the book. VINS Research Coordinator Annette Gosnell has aided the work on the book in many ways. Nancy L. Martin of the VINS staff, is responsible for the line drawings and excellent maps, as well as for many long hours of editing and lay-out of the manuscript. Lastly, I am indebted to VINS Director Sarah B. Laughlin for her unflagging support and hard work on this project; without her it might never have gotten off the ground.

W.G.E.

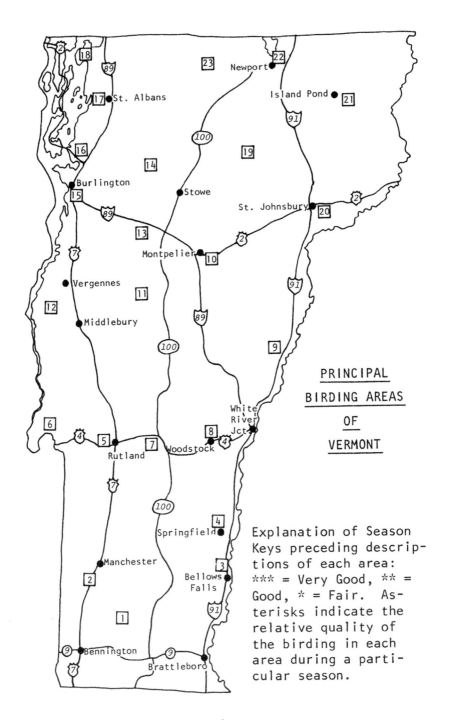

PRINCIPAL
BIRDING AREAS
OF
VERMONT

Explanation of Season
Keys preceding descrip-
tions of each area:
*** = Very Good, ** =
Good, * = Fair. As-
terisks indicate the
relative quality of
the birding in each
area during a parti-
cular season.

CONTENTS

White-winged Crossbills

INTRODUCTION

Any account involving the birds of Vermont must take in a great diversity of birds. About 330 species of birds have been recorded in Vermont. Of this total, about 250 species occur on an annual basis, with slightly less than 200 of these breeding within the state. From what has been written about Vermont, one might get the impression that the state is covered with mountains and unremittingly cold. While this is not far from correct, the state is considerably more diverse than that account allows.

Vermont may be conveniently divided into seven physiographic regions. These are: 1. the Green Mountains, 2. the Taconic Mountains, 3. the Valley of Vermont, 4. the Eastern Foothills, 5. the Connecticut Valley, 6. the Champlain Lowlands, and 7. the Northeastern Highlands, also known as the Northeast Kingdom.

Since Vermont is nicknamed "the Green Mountain State" it seems fitting to describe this region of the state first. The Green Mountains bisect the state vertically from the Canadian border to the Massachusetts state line. The state's highest mountains are found in the range. These mountains are largely composed of metamorphosed pre-Cambrian and Cambrian sedimentary rock. The Green Mountains are part of the larger Appalachian Mountain System and were created some 500 million years ago in the Ordovician Period. The mountains form a barrier to weather from the west and wring from the passing clouds the highest annual rate of precipitation in Vermont. The high altitudes of the mountains make for cool summer temperatures and average January temperatures of ten degrees Farenheit or less. In northern Vermont, the Green Mountains take the form of a main ridge and one to two front ranges. Some of the more noteworthy front ranges are the Worcester Range, the Lowell Mountains, the Cold Hollow Mountains, and the Northfield Range. The main

1

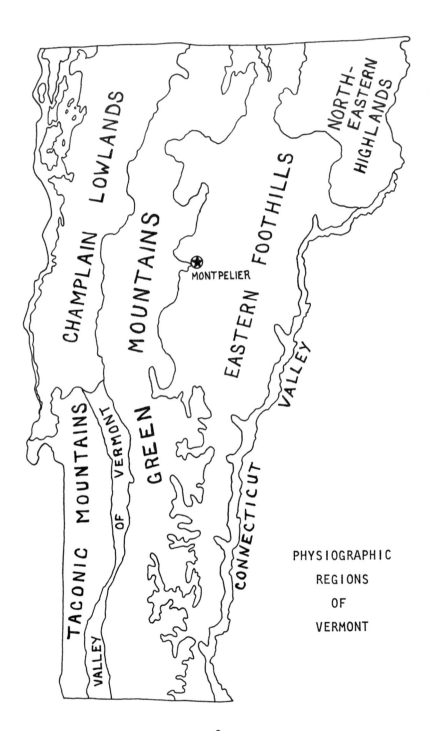

TACONIC MOUNTAINS

VALLEY OF VERMONT

CHAMPLAIN LOWLANDS

GREEN MOUNTAINS

MONTPELIER

CONNECTICUT VALLEY

EASTERN FOOTHILLS

NORTH-EASTERN HIGHLANDS

PHYSIOGRAPHIC
REGIONS
OF
VERMONT

2

ridge of the Green Mountains in the north includes such prominent peaks as Mt. Abraham, Mt. Ellen, Camel's Hump, Mt. Mansfield (the state's highest mountain), and Jay Peak. The southern Green Mountains form a broad plateau averaging over 2,500 feet above sea level at the center. The highest mountains in this portion of the range are Glastonbury, Mt. Snow, Stratton Mountain, Killington Peak, and Pico Peak. Most of the higher ridges are covered with a stunted sub-alpine forest of Balsam Fir and Red Spruce. One species of bird is unique to this habitat in Vermont, the Bicknell's race of the Grey-cheeked Thrush, a relict of glacial times. Other typical species of this habitat are Yellow-bellied Flycatcher, Winter Wren, Swainson's Thrush, Golden-crowned Kinglet, Nashville, Magnolia, Yellow-rumped, Blackpoll (very common), and Canada Warblers, Northern Junco, and White-throated Sparrow. Two of Vermont's mountains, Camel's Hump and Mt. Mansfield, are exposed enough to have treelines and limited alpine flora. The slopes of the mountains are cloaked with northern hardwoods, a forest type which covers most of Vermont's mountains and hills. The principal trees of this forest are Sugar Maple, Beech, Yellow Birch, and Eastern Hemlock.

To avoid unnecessary repetition, the typical birds of northern hardwood forest are enumerated in list form here. These are, by and large, the regular breeding residents of the forest land of Vermont.

Broad-winged Hawk	Least Flycatcher
Red-shouldered Hawk	Eastern Pewee
(near beaver ponds)	Blue Jay
Ruffed Grouse	Black-capped Chickadee
Barred Owl	White-breasted Nuthatch
Pileated Woodpecker	Brown Creeper
Yellow-bellied Sapsucker	(prefers hemlock)
Hairy Woodpecker	Winter Wren
Downy Woodpecker	Wood Thrush
Great Crested Flycatcher	Hermit Thrush

Veery
Solitary Vireo (hemlock)
Red-eyed Vireo
Black-and-white Warbler
Black-throated Blue
  Warbler
Black-throated Green
  Warbler
Blackburnian Warbler
  (spruce, hemlock)

Ovenbird
Louisiana Waterthrush
  (along streams below
  2,000 feet)
Mourning Warbler
  (slash/brushy clearings)
Canada Warbler
American Redstart
Scarlet Tanager
Rose-breasted Grosbeak

The second major mountain range in Vermont is the Taconic Range. This range occupies the south-western portion of the state. These are steep mountains with a network of deep valleys running between them. Among the streams that cut valleys through this range are the Poultney River, the Mettawee River, the Battenkill and the Hoosic River. The principal bedrock of the region consists of slate and marble indicating an oceanic origin for the region's rocks. The forests of the Taconics are largely northern hardwood, but there is some oak-hickory woodland on the lower mountains and in the valleys. The higher peaks of the range clear 3,000 feet with the tallest mountains, Equinox and Dorset, exceeding 3,800 feet. On these higher peaks there is a similar sub-alpine forest to that of the Green Mountains. Another important habitat of the Taconics is wetland. There are small marshes bordering many of the larger lakes in the region and there is an excellent, large cattail marsh in the valley of the Castleton River (the West Rutland Marsh). Due to the high incidence of oak and hickory, both of which provide excellent mast, the Taconics represent the center of the recently reclaimed range of the Wild Turkey in the state.

A small region which lies between the Green Mountains and the Taconics is the Valley of Vermont. This narrow, rolling valley is an extension of the lowlands surrounding Lake Champlain. The farmlands, overgrown pastures, and forest edge of this region

4

have bird life similar to much of the open country of the state. Some representative species are listed here.

Turkey Vulture	Cedar Waxwing
Red-tailed Hawk	Starling
American Kestrel	Yellow-throated Vireo
Killdeer	Warbling Vireo
American Woodcock	Yellow Warbler
(wet ground)	Chestnut-sided Warbler
Rock Dove	Common Yellowthroat
Mourning Dove	House Sparrow
Black-billed Cuckoo	Bobolink
Ruby-throated Hummingbird	Eastern Meadowlark
Common Flicker	Red-winged Blackbird
Eastern Kingbird	Northern Oriole
Eastern Phoebe	Common Grackle
(near water)	Brown-headed Cowbird
Tree Swallow	Northern Cardinal
Barn Swallow	(low elevations)
Cliff Swallow	Indigo Bunting
American Crow	American Goldfinch
House Wren	Rufous-sided Towhee
Grey Catbird	Savannah Sparrow
Brown Thrasher	Vesper Sparrow
American Robin	Chipping Sparrow
Eastern Bluebird	Field Sparrow
(local)	Song Sparrow

The Eastern Foothills are a diverse region of hills and valleys extending from Newport in the north to Brattleboro in southern Vermont. The landscape is generally rough, and there is a wide array of habitats depending upon the vagaries of local climatic and topographic conditions. The most common forest type is the familiar northern hardwoods, but cool pockets, bogs, and higher elevations have thick spruce-fir woodland. There are many lakes and ponds in the Eastern Foothills, particularly in the north. These offer migratory and nesting habitat to a few waterbirds. The species previously described for forest and farmland habitats are also found in the region, with some species becoming scarce in the northern portion of the region. Examples of this distribution include Turkey Vulture, Brown Thrasher, Yellow-throated Vireo, Louisiana Waterthrush, Northern Cardinal, and Rufous-sided Towhee.

The Connecticut Valley is not generally considered a separate physiographic region from the Eastern Foothills and the Northeastern Highlands, but it has certain characteristics which set its fauna apart from the adjoining regions. The most important factor separating this region's avifauna from the adjacent Eastern Foothills' is that the river valley represents both an important migratory corridor and a narrow intrusion of more southerly climatic conditions. The river opens in late March or early April, ahead of the lakes and ponds in the eastern part of the state, and floods regularly in late April. The valley is, therefore, very good for waterfowl migrations during spring. The valley is also a major route for small landbirds in April, May, September, and October. The valley represents a gateway for southern bird species which reach the northern edge of their range in Vermont. Such species as Turkey Vulture, Willow Flycatcher, Tufted Titmouse, Northern Mockingbird, Blue-grey Gnatcatcher, Pine and Prairie Warblers occur in higher numbers in the southern Connecticut Valley than in the adjacent backcountry.

The Champlain Lowlands are radically different than the other regions of the state in physical appearance. The lands next to Lake Champlain are either flat or gently rolling in character. The bedrock of the region is sedimentary and calcareous, and the soils are deep and favorable for farming. These factors combine to create a landscape of open farmland with scattered woodlots of hardwoods, including significant stands of oak and hickory. The streams of the lowlands are meandering and are surrounded by cattail marshes and swamps of Silver Maple, Swamp White Oak, and Cottonwood. The large acreage of wetland habitat assures that the Champlain Lowlands are the major breeding grounds and migratory resting place for waterbirds in Vermont. Recognizing this, wildlife management authorities at the state and federal levels have established five major state Wildlife Management Areas and one National Wildlife Refuge in the region. The climate of the area is both warmer and drier than the other regions of the state. New York's Adirondacks form a rain shadow which causes the rainfall in the low-lands to fall below 30 inches per annum in several locations. The lake has the effect of ameliorating the temperatures of the area except when it is frozen. The farmlands of the region support a num-ber of breeding species which are unique to, or at their most common in, the Champlain Lowlands. Among these are numbered Northern Harrier, Grey Partridge (Grand Isle County), Upland Sandpiper, Common Screech Owl, Red-headed Woodpecker (very local), Horned Lark, Purple Martin, and Grasshopper Sparrow (Ad-dison County). The wetlands harbor such nesting species as Pied-billed Grebe, Great Blue Heron, Least Bittern (uncommon), American Bittern, Canada Goose (Dead Creek), Mallard, American Black Duck, Blue-winged Teal, Wood Duck, Virginia Rail, Sora, Common Gallinule, Black Tern, and Marsh Wren. There are major bird colonies on some of the islands in Lake Champlain which support breeding populations of Cattle Egret, Black-crowned Night Heron, Herring Gull, Ring-billed Gull, and Common Tern. The lake and adjacent wetlands host large numbers of migra-tory waterbirds, including significant numbers of shorebirds.

Last but certainly not least are the Northeast-ern Highlands of Essex and eastern Orleans Counties. This region is an extension into Vermont of the Mes-ozoic Granitic Dome which forms the White Mountains of New Hampshire. Underlying granite causes the soil to be acidic, favoring conifers and some mixed northern hardwood forest. The high latitude and average high altitude (the average elevation of the

7

Island Pond Quadrangle is 2,136 feet) make the region as cool in summer as the Green Mountains and every bit as frigid in winter. Boreal forest makes up a considerable portion of the woodland habitat of the area. With this habitat comes an avifauna which is largely specific to this region of the state. Some of the principal breeding species of the spruce-fir forests of the Northeastern Highlands are Northern Goshawk, Spruce Grouse (rare), Black-backed Three-toed Woodpecker, Yellow-bellied and Olive-sided Flycatchers, Grey Jay, Northern Raven, Boreal Chickadee, Red-breasted Nuthatch, Winter Wren, Hermit and Swainson's Thrushes, Golden-crowned and Ruby-crowned Kinglets, Solitary Vireo, Nashville, Northern Parula, Magnolia, Cape May (uncommon), Yellow-rumped and Canada Warblers, Rusty Blackbird (uncommon), Northern Junco, and White-throated and Lincoln's Sparrows. Many of these species are not confined to the northeast but are also found in suitable habitat elsewhere in Vermont. Some, such as Rusty Blackbird, Ruby-crowned Kinglet, Black-backed Three-toed Woodpecker, and Lincoln's Sparrow, are otherwise found only in the Green Mountains, especially on the broad plateau of the southern range.

The best times for observing birds in the state are spring and autumn, when the widest variety of species is seen. The peak months of spring migration are April for waterfowl and hawks and May for small landbirds and shorebirds. May is a particularly good time for birding, with most of the resident breeding birds returning to Vermont and migrants passing through the state to their Canadian nesting grounds. Apple blossom time in combination with an early morning songbird chorus is a marvelous experience. During autumn, September and October offer the best birding, as well as an exciting foliage display.

In the past, the breeding season was overlooked as a productive time for birding. With the advent of the Vermont Breeding Bird Atlas, this is no longer

true. Most birds are encountered to best advantage
in the breeding season. With a total of a little
less than 200 breeding species, the state offers a
wide variety of birdlife to the summer traveler.

Winter is a time of climatic extremes in Vermont, with heavy snow, biting cold, and occasional
wild upward swings in temperature thrown in for variety. Much of Vermont is a forbidding place for a
bird attempting to survive the rigors of this cold-
est and bleakest of seasons. A little better than
160 species of birds have been found during winter
in Vermont, of which a little over 100 are seen each
winter. Some species such as Rough-legged Hawk,
Glaucous and Iceland Gulls, Snowy Owl, Bohemian
Waxwing, Northern Shrike, Pine Grosbeak, American
Tree Sparrow, and Snow Bunting are found largely as
winter visitors to the state. When planning a visit
to the Green Mountain State in winter, it is a wise
procedure to write the Vermont Institute of Natural
Science or any of the thirteen Christmas Count com-
pilers regarding birding in the various regions of
the state; a stamped self-addressed envelope is a
must when requesting information.

When traveling, everyone needs a place to lay
his or her head. Accommodations in Vermont range
from deluxe resorts to primitive campsites. This
being a tourist state, I have not included specific
directions to hotels and motels in the accounts de-
scribing birding areas. Most sections of the state
have an ample supply of hotels, motels, and cabins
for the traveler. A good procedure would be to write
ahead to the Agency of Development and Community Af-
fairs, Vermont Travel Division, 61 Elm Street, Montpelier, Vermont 05602, or the Vermont State Cham-
ber of Commerce, Box 37, Montpelier, Vermont
05602 for information regarding lodging around the
state. There are several excellent state, National
Forest, and private campgrounds. Some of these are
mentioned in the text. Especially recommended are
the camping areas in state forests and parks.

Write to the Department of Forests, Parks, and Rec-
reation, Montpelier, Vermont 05602 for exact opening
and closing dates of individual state camping areas.

As with the other humid parts of North America,
Vermont has its fair share of noxious biting insects.
These critters occur in distinct seasons. Black
flies are prevalent from late May to mid-June; mos-
quitoes are at their most vicious from early June to
early July; and deer flies (anything but dear) are
noisome from mid-June to late July. Be prepared for
these beasts with proper clothing and insect repel-
lents. Also, be careful of Poison Ivy, the only
troublesome plant at this latitude (other than
thorns). The only part of the state where one can
almost count on not encountering this plant is the
Northeastern Highlands. Only one species of poison-
ous snake is found in Vermont, and it is very rare,
having been unfortunately destroyed on sight for
generations. Among the areas described in the text
of this book the Timber Rattlesnake is found with
regularity only in West Haven.

A few cautionary notes for birders are in order
here. First, whenever possible, the birding areas
mentioned in the text are public; however, much of
Vermont is privately owned. When birding on private
property, use common courtesy and obey signs. Secondly, all state fishing accesses are maintained
primarily for fishermen. Do not interfere with
their activities when birding in these areas. Lastly, to avoid coming to grief under rolling wheels,
check freight train schedules and keep alert for
trains when using railroad rights-of-way.

A word about the nomenclature used in this book
is also in order here. The English names used in
this book are the standardized names developed by
the American Ornithologists' Union (AOU) Checklist
Committee in the 1957 AOU Checklist and its supple-
ments with the exception of a few species. The revised names of these species are used in the 1980

10

edition of Peterson's A Field Guide to the Birds of
Eastern and Central North America and the ABA Checklist, published by the American Birding Association,
Box 4335, Austin, Texas 78765. These changes are
expected to be adopted when the AOU publishes its
fully revised checklist in 1983. The name changes
put into effect since the publication of Robbin's
Golden Guide in 1966 are listed below.

NEW NAME	OLD NAME
Great Egret	Common Egret
Snow Goose	Blue Goose
(Blue Goose now a color form)	
American Black Duck	Black Duck
Common Pintail	Pintail
American Wigeon	American Widgeon
Northern Shoveler	Shoveler
Northern Harrier	Marsh Hawk
Merlin	Pigeon Hawk
American Kestrel	Sparrow Hawk
Lesser Golden Plover	American Golden Plover
Upland Sandpiper	Upland Plover
Red Knot	Knot
Common Screech Owl	Screech Owl
Common Flicker	Yellow-shafted Flicker
Willow Flycatcher	Traill's Flycatcher ("fitz-bew" birds)
Alder Flycatcher	Traill's Flycatcher ("fee-be'o" birds)
Eastern Pewee	Eastern Wood Pewee
Northern Raven	Common Raven
American Crow	Common Crow
Marsh Wren	Long-billed Marsh Wren
Sedge Wren	Short-billed Marsh Wren
Northern Mockingbird	Mockingbird
Grey Catbird	Catbird
Northern Parula	Parula Warbler
Yellow-rumped Warbler	Myrtle Warbler
Northern Oriole	Baltimore Oriole
Northern Cardinal	Cardinal
Northern Junco	Slate-colored Junco
American Tree Sparrow	Tree Sparrow

11

1. THE SOUTHERN GREEN MOUNTAINS

Season Key: Spring **
              Summer ***
              Autumn **

Recommended Time to Visit: May 1 - October 31

    As was noted in the introduction, the Green
Mountains of southern Vermont have a very different
topography from the northern Green Mountains. The
broad, high plateau of the southern Green Mountains
hosts birdlife similar to the northern portions of
the range. There are, however, some significant
differences between the north and south. The average high elevation of the southern Green Mountains
in combination with an abundance of glacial ponds
and beaver meadows creates excellent boreal habitat
for some species of birds which are scarce or absent
from the northern part of the Green Mountain range.
Among these species are Black-backed Three-toed
Woodpecker, Ruby-crowned Kinglet, Rusty Blackbird,
and Lincoln's Sparrow.

    Some of the more accessible areas in the south-
ern Green Mountains are along Route 9, the Molly
Stark Highway, which links Brattleboro to Bennington. A good place to acquaint oneself with the
birds of this region is Molly Stark State Park, 15
miles west of Brattleboro and 25 miles east of Bennington. Three and one-half miles west of the park
is the year round resort community of Wilmington.
The park offers campsites and lean-tos in season.
The best birding in the park is along the 1.7 mile
loop trail on Mt. Olga which originates and ends at
the camping area. The trail to the summit of this
2,415 foot mountain passes through northern hardwood
forest on the ascent and thick young evergreens on
its descent. On the top there is a fire tower offering excellent views of southern Vermont and adjacent Massachusetts. Some of the birds which may
be encountered are Ruffed Grouse, Barred Owl, Yel-

low-bellied Sapsucker, Red-breasted Nuthatch, Wood, Hermit and Swainson's Thrushes, Solitary Vireo, Magnolia, Black-throated Blue, Yellow-rumped, Black-throated Green and Blackburnian Warblers, and Scarlet Tanager and Rose-breasted Grosbeak. The fire tower and the lookout maintained at the base of the Hogback Mountain Ski Area (a mile east of the park) are good for viewing autumn hawk flights.

North of Wilmington the summits and connecting ridge of Mt. Snow (3,556 feet) and Haystack Mountain (3,420 feet) are excellent for sub-alpine birdlife. The summit of Haystack Mountain may be reached by a relatively moderate climb up a well-maintained trail. To reach this trail, proceed west from Wilmington on Route 9 for 1.1 miles and turn right onto Haystack Road where there is a prominent sign indicating the Chimney Hill second home development. Continue on this road, taking a left onto Chimney Hill Road at 1.2 miles. Take the next right onto Binney Brook Road and proceed past Howe's Loop (both the lower

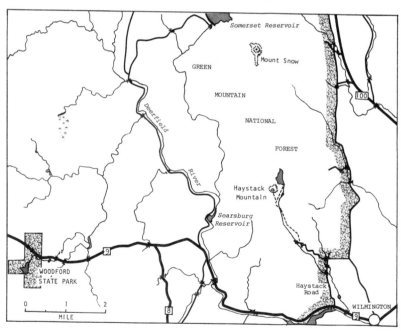

and upper ends), Large Maple Way, and Lila Lane.
Turn right at the T intersection with Twin Chimney
Road and turn left at the next intersection onto Upper Dam Road. The trail is on the right just beyond
the second road on the right. Park at a nearby widening in the road. The trail is marked by a brown
sign with yellow and orange arrows. The initial
stages of the trail pass through hardwood forest
with similar birds to Mt. Olga. At .7 of a mile
there is a fork in the trail; the left fork continues to the summit in .6 of a mile and the right fork
proceeds to Haystack Pond, a beautiful high elevation lake with a few Rusty Blackbirds and Ruby-
crowned Kinglets. The stunted spruces and firs of
the summit harbor such characteristic montane birds
as Yellow-bellied Flycatcher, Swainson's and Grey-
cheeked Thrushes, and Blackpoll Warbler.

Five and a half miles west of Wilmington the
Somerset Reservoir Road turns north from Route 9 and
winds 9 miles through the mountains to this four and
a half mile long body of water. Some of the birds
the observer might expect on the way in to the reservoir are Spotted Sandpiper, Pileated Woodpecker,
Alder and Olive-sided Flycatchers, Hermit and
Swainson's Thrushes, Golden-crowned Kinglet, Solitary Vireo, and Nashville, Northern Parula, Magnolia, Black-throated Blue, Yellow-rumped, Black-
throated Green, Blackburnian, Mourning and Canada
Warblers. The reservoir itself should occasionally
have migratory waterbirds and sometimes hosts summering Common Loons and Common Mergansers.

Another state park on Route 9, 10 miles west
of Wilmington and 11 miles east of Bennington, is
Woodford State Park. As with Molly Stark, there is
camping in season with both lean-tos and campsites
offered. At 2,400 feet, the camping area is the
highest in the state park system. Birding the forests of the park and around Adams Reservoir should
be productive with much the same representation of
species as Molly Stark State Park.

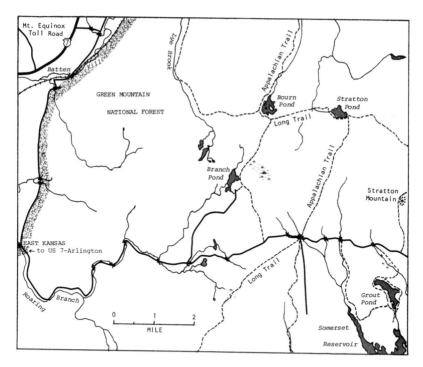

The next important road over the southern Green
Mountains is the unpaved highway maintained by the
National Forest Service between West Wardsboro and
East Arlington. This road may be reached from Route
7 in Arlington by turning east and passing through
East Arlington, Kansas, and East Kansas, and following the Roaring Branch uphill. From the east, turn
off Route 100 in West Wardsboro at the sign indicating the town of Stratton. West of Stratton the
road climbs to the top of the plateau of the Green
Mountains. The breeding birds of this region include American Black Duck, Hooded Merganser (uncommon), Broad-winged Hawk, Red-tailed Hawk, Ruffed
Grouse, Chimney Swift, Pileated Woodpecker, Yellow-
bellied Sapsucker, Yellow-bellied, Alder and Olive-
sided Flycatchers, Northern Raven, Red-breasted Nuthatch, Winter Wren, Wood, Hermit and Swainson's
Thrushes, Golden and Ruby-crowned Kinglets (the latter around ponds), Nashville, Northern Parula (local), Magnolia, Black-throated Blue, Yellow-rumped,

Black-throated Green, Blackburnian, Blackpoll and
Canada Warblers, Northern Waterthrush, Rusty Blackbird (ponds), Lincoln's (brushy clearings and beaver
ponds), and Swamp Sparrows (pond edge). In addition
to these species the Black-backed Three-toed Woodpecker appears to be resident in the area with nesting in 1979 at Branch Pond and suspected breeding in
1980 at Bourn Pond.

Major points of interest in this area are
Branch, Bourn, and Stratton Ponds and Stratton Mountain. The head of the Stratton Mountain Trail is
5.2 miles west of West Wardsboro and 15 miles east
of East Arlington. The trail is indicated by a blue
sign; there is parking for the trail west of the
sign on the north side of the road. A tenth of a
mile north of the road is the Webster Shelter, with
space to sleep seven. The South Peak of Stratton
(3,936 feet) is reached after a hike of 2.7 miles
from the Arlington-West Wardsboro Highway. There is
a fire tower on the summit, which is one of only two
manned towers in the entire state. The summit and
upper slopes are covered with a stunted forest of
spruce and fir which harbors typical high elevation
birdlife. Both Bourn and Stratton Ponds must be
reached by hiking. Stratton Pond lies 2 miles beyond the South Peak of Stratton Mountain via the
Stratton Mountain Trail. One may also reach Stratton Pond by hiking on the Long/Appalachian Trail
from the Arlington/West Wardsboro Highway for 4.5
miles. Bourn Pond is 1.8 miles beyond the outlet
of Stratton Pond. To reach Branch Pond one may take
the Branch Pond Trail which lies 1 mile west of the
Long Trail and proceeds north for 1.9 miles to the
short side trail to the pond. The pond may also be
reached by driving north for 2.5 miles on a National
Forest fire road (the only prominent turn to the
north between East Kansas and Stratton village) to
the edge of the Lye Brook Wilderness Area. Branch
Pond lies at the boundary of the wilderness area.
At the parking lot at the end of the road there is a
trail on the left which proceeds .2 of a mile to

Lincoln's Sparrow

MARTIN

the south end of the pond. Ahead and a little to
the right of the lot is a trail which reaches the
shore of the pond after about a one half mile walk.

One may also reach Bourn Pond via this trail by
continuing north on the blue-blazed Branch Pond
Trail for 1.8 miles. The Green Mountain Club main-
tains overnight camping facilities on both Bourn and
Stratton Ponds. For more detailed descriptions of
the trails in this area, one should obtain the
Guidebook of the Long Trail from the Green Mountain
Club of Montpelier.

Another good area accessible from Route 30 in
Bondville is the area surrounding Gale Meadows Pond.
The pond may be reached by taking the dirt road off
Route 30 which runs past the Bondville Town Hall.
The pond is reached after a two mile trip. The area
is very popular as a fishing spot. The countryside
around the pond has a fine selection of breeding
birds. One local observer has noted 121 species of
breeding birds in this area since the mid 1960's.
Among these have been Common Loon, American Bittern,
Hooded and Common Mergansers, Northern Goshawk, Coop-
er's and Red-shouldered Hawks, American Woodcock,
Common Snipe, Saw-whet Owl, Black-backed Three-toed
Woodpecker (a nest in 1969), Rough-winged Swallow,
Philadelphia Vireo, Tennessee Warbler (fledglings in
1981), both Northern and Louisiana Waterthrushes,
Rusty Blackbird and Red Crossbill.

2. MANCHESTER-ARLINGTON AREA

Season Key: Spring ***
Summer **
Autumn ***
Winter *

Recommended Time to Visit: April 1 - November 30

Manchester and Arlington lie in the Marble Valley or, more properly, the Valley of Vermont, the flat, narrow valley which lies between the Green and Taconic Mountains. The major commercial enterprises of this region are dairy farming and tourism. Skiing is important to Manchester, with the Bromley and Stratton areas both nearby. The Taconics, featuring 3,816 foot Mount Equinox and 3,804 foot Dorset Peak dominate the western skyline. The Green Mountains present a sheer wall rising to 2,500 feet above sea level on the east.

Eight miles north of Manchester on U.S. Route 7 is Emerald Lake State Park, encompassing 400 acres of woodland and lake. The park offers camping with campsites and lean-tos from Memorial Day to Labor Day. There are nature trails, boat rentals, and a swimming beach. The area is very good for birding during migration, especially in spring. A wide variety of small landbirds follows the Valley of Vermont during migration and the rich woodlands along the lake are attractive to transients. During summer the park features such breeding species as Barred Owl, Least and Great Crested Flycatchers, Eastern Pewee, Winter Wren, Wood Thrush, Yellow-throated and Warbling Vireos, Black-throated Blue, Black-throated Green and Blackburnian Warblers, Louisiana Waterthrush, Scarlet Tanager and Rose-breasted Grosbeak.

Another good area is Mount Equinox, the highest peak in the Taconic Range. A good way to bird the mountain is to hike up the trail from Manchester.

This affords the birder a chance to sample the bird-life of the mountain from base to summit. Another method of reaching the top is to drive the toll road to the summit.

The hiking trail is reached from U.S. Route 7 in Manchester by proceeding west on Seminary Road, 1.1 miles south of the intersection of Routes 7 and 11 in Manchester Center. Bear right past Burr and Burton Academy. Park beside the academy's athletic fields; the trail starts on the opposite side of the fields. The trail is steep and requires a good deal of energy. The route is marked by blue blazes and reaches the summit after 2.9 miles. On the lower slopes, the observer will encounter typical birds of northern hardwood forest. Above 3,500 feet the bird-life is similar to the same habitats of stunted spruce and fir in the Green Mountains. The toll road is reached by proceeding south from Manchester on Route 7 for three miles. The road proceeds up-hill from a gate house on the right hand side of the road. There is a complex of gift shops around the entrance making it hard to miss.

The village of Arlington lies seven miles south of Manchester on Route 7. Besides good inns and motels, there are two privately owned camping areas in this small town. The better of the two for birding is Howell's Camping Area, which is reached via School Street, the first left off Route 313 west in Arlington. To bird here one must be a camper. There is pine and hardwood forest around the area, but the main attractions of this spot are the small ponds along the campground road. The cattail marsh and pond edges here are good for Great Blue Heron, Green Heron, American Black Duck, Wood Duck, Virginia Rail, Common Gallinule, Belted Kingfisher, Yellow-throated Vireo, and Swamp Sparrow. The area is also good during migration.

Three and a half miles south of Arlington off Route 7-A is Shaftsbury Lake State Park. The park is

the first left off Route 7-A after crossing the
Shaftsbury town line. The park includes 101 acres of
forest and lakeshore around 27 acre Shaftsbury Lake.
There are picnic facilities, a nature trail, and a
swimming beach here. There is also camping by ar-
rangement for organized groups. The park is best
for birding during migration, when large numbers of
flycatchers, thrushes, kinglets, vireos, warblers,
and sparrows may be seen. The unexpected is always
a possibility, as a recent record of Worm-eating
Warbler indicates. The lake is also worth checking
for migratory waterbirds.

3. HERRICK'S COVE

Season Key: Spring ***
               Summer *
               Autumn ***

Recommended Time to Visit: April 1 - December 10

     The valley of the Connecticut River is one of
the two major migration corridors in Vermont. Waterfowl migration, particularly, is confined to
these two corridors, as there is little attractive
habitat between the river and the very fine Champlain Valley flyway. The Connecticut River Valley
also offers a fine north-south route for small
landbirds and usually plays host to healthy spring
and autumn flights. During these periods of migration, the Herrick's Cove area in Rockingham stands
without peer as a resting area for most of the migratory species of the valley.

     Herrick's Cove is best reached from Exit 6 off
Interstate Route 91. From the exit, proceed to the
intersection of Vermont Route 103 and U.S. Route 5.
Turn onto Route 5 north. You will soon pass over
the Green Mountain Railroad and Williams River in
quick succession. Continue for another .4 of a

mile, passing a mobile home park on the right. Directly beyond the mobile home park bear right onto a narrow paved road. On the right as you proceed on this road will be a large expanse of open water. This is Herrick's Cove, which encompasses the mouth and delta of the Williams River.

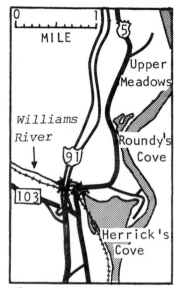

Stop at a pull-off a short way up the road and check the open water and the small enclosed bay near the road for Pied-billed Grebe, Great Blue and Green Herons, Canada Goose, Mallard, American Black, Wood and Ring-necked Ducks, Common Goldeneye, Bufflehead, Common Merganser, Osprey, Belted Kingfisher, Solitary Sandpiper (during May and also from August-September), and Spotted Sandpiper. In April and early May, migratory swallows of five species are often abundant, skimming over the surface of the cove. Nearly every duck recorded in Vermont may be seen here during migration. Examples of rarities that have been seen include Eurasian Wigeon, Barrow's Goldeneye, and Ruddy Duck. Continue on, bearing left to a boat ramp along the Connecticut River. Scan the river for ducks and the heavens for soaring raptors (principally Osprey, Turkey Vulture, and Red-tailed Hawk). Check the pine plantation for owls and migrants. Proceed from here on foot into the NEPCO picnic area (complete with very primitive facilities) on the right. Check the brush along the various roadways for migratory landbirds. This area is particularly good for sparrows in April and October and is very reliable for Palm Warbler in early spring and late autumn. Blue-grey Gnatcatchers are now found regularly in the area. Continue to check both the river and the cove from various viewpoints, as a hidden waterbird of interest may turn up at any of these spots. Upon reaching the southern end of the picnic area, proceed onto the point via a narrow path. The point offers another good view of the water and sometimes acts as a small scale migrant trap.

Retrace your steps to your car and return to Route 5. Proceed north on Route 5 for about three-quarters of a mile, pulling off at the second turn-off on the right. This spot affords a commanding view of the Connecticut River and Roundy's Cove. A check here is usually worthwhile as there are often Canada Geese, Snow Geese, Wood and Ring-necked Ducks, Hooded Merganser, and various other ducks here during migration.

Continue north on Route 5 for almost a mile, taking the next right. On the observer's right is the region of the Upper Meadows, a huge floodplain area about half of which is farmed with the rest dotted with small oxbow lakes and floodplain forest. This area, when carefully explored, often proves as rich as Herrick's Cove itself. The fields are good, in season, for shorebirds, sparrows, Water Pipit (April-May, September-October), Horned Lark, Snow Bunting (November-March), blackbirds and various raptors. The riparian woodlands are excellent for small landbirds during migration and shelter nesting Blue-grey Gnatcatchers. The oxbows are worth checking for ducks (especially Wood Duck) and herons. Parking may be a problem here; one should ask permission to park along the road or to use the field roads which provide the best access to this area. It is best not to attempt to use these roads when they are muddy.

Snow Buntings

4. SPRINGFIELD AREA

Season Key: Spring ***
              Summer **
              Autumn **

Recommended Time to Visit: March 30 - December 1

      Springfield lies at the heart of the "precision valley" named for the major industry of this small city, precision tool manufacturing. The Black River and Connecticut River Valleys provide good waterfowl habitat during migration. The northern hardwood forests which cover the hills surrounding the city harbor the typical nesting birds of east-central Vermont.

      Start at the center of town on Routes 106/11 and proceed northwest to the junction where the routes divide. Continue on Route 106 north at the traffic signal for about 2.5 miles. At the west end

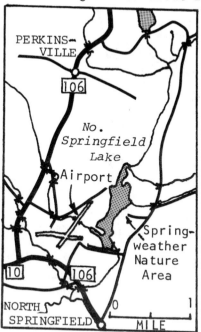

of the village of North Springfield, turn right onto a paved road marked by a sign indicating the North Springfield Dam. You will arrive at a causeway traversing the top of the large earthen dam after about .75 of a mile. The dam backs up a 1.2 mile long lake along the valley of the Black River. At the middle of the causeway there is room to pull off and scan the open water. During migration one may see ducks and other waterbirds here. Most commonly seen are Mallard, American Black Duck, Common Merganser,

23

Osprey (overhead or perched in lakeside trees),
Spotted Sandpiper, and Belted Kingfisher.

After crossing the causeway, turn left onto a
paved road which parallels the lake and continue for
another .6 of a mile. On the left the observer will
note a prominent sign announcing the Springweather
Nature Area. This area, administered by the Ascutney Mountain Audubon Society, includes 70 acres of
upland and riparian habitat along North Springfield
Lake. Turn left and drive down the hill. At the
bottom there is a parking area on the right. By far
the best way to observe birds here is on foot. One
may walk the roadways maintained by the Army Corps
of Engineers or the fine trails established by Ascutney Mountain Audubon along the lake. During waterfowl migration the best viewing may be had by
taking the trail through the field to the west (see
map) to the hemlock-crowned bluff overlooking the
lake. Waterfowl commonly seen include Canada Goose,
Mallard, American Black Duck, Blue-winged and Green-

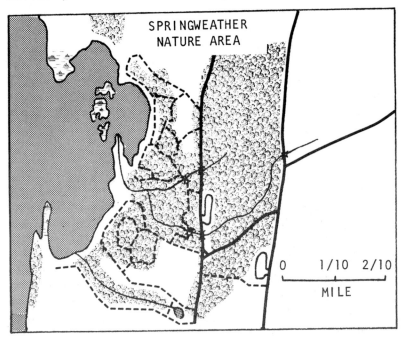

SPRINGWEATHER
NATURE AREA

0   1/10   2/10

MILE

winged Teal, Wood Duck, Ring-necked Duck, and Common Merganser. Other species occur from time to time. This area is also good for Green and Great Blue Herons, Osprey, American Woodcock, Spotted Sandpiper, and Belted Kingfisher. Transient shorebirds are seen in May and from August to October. The woods of the preserve are good for landbird migrants. A morning here in spring or autumn would be well spent. The best location for migrant warblers is at the north end of the gravel road (beyond the parking area). Just before the road dead-ends, there is thick second growth which is excellent for up to 20 species of warblers on a given day. Nesting species include American Woodcock, American Kestrel, Ruffed Grouse, Killdeer, Spotted Sandpiper, Mourning Dove, Black-billed Cuckoo, Ruby-throated Hummingbird, Common Flicker, Great Crested Flycatcher, Least Flycatcher, Eastern Pewee, White-breasted Nuthatch, Brown Creeper, Wood Thrush, Veery, Eastern Bluebird, Blue-grey Gnatcatcher (nest in 1981), Solitary and Red-eyed Vireos, Black-and-white, Yellow, Chestnut-sided and Black-throated Green Warblers, Common Yellowthroat, Ovenbird, American Redstart, Scarlet Tanager, Rose-breasted Grosbeak, Indigo Bunting, Vesper, Field, Chipping and White-throated Sparrows. Ascutney Mountain Audubon has recorded 156 species in the area as of 1981.

Return to the main road, turn left, and proceed for about 3 miles, bearing left to follow the main road. During waterfowl migration check the area along the Black River and Stoughton Pond for ducks. Proceed for another .8 of a mile to Route 106. Turn left and continue on, passing through the village of Perkinsville. After 2.2 miles turn left at a sign indicating the Springfield Airport. The airport may be good during spring and autumn for American Kestrel, Killdeer, Horned Lark, Eastern Meadowlark, Indigo Bunting, Savannah and Vesper Sparrows. Occasionally an unusual shorebird has been seen here in autumn (e.g. Lesser Golden Plover and Upland Sandpiper).

Upon leaving the airport, take Route 106 back into Springfield and proceed out of town on Route 11 east. Pass under Interstate 91 and continue until reaching the Charlestown, New Hampshire, toll bridge. Turn right into the state maintained fishing access at the mouth of the Black River. Although this area is usually worth a quick check, it is generally not productive. Return to Route 11 and proceed north on Route 5. After approximately 1.5 miles the observer will note a huge rolling floodplain cornfield on the right. These are the Springfield Meadows. This area is particularly good from early to late April in wet years when the low places in the fields become extensively flooded. Geese and almost all of the "marsh ducks" which migrate through the Connecticut Valley may be seen here during such times. These include Canada and Snow Geese, Mallard, American Black Duck, Common Pintail, both teal, Gadwall, American Wigeon, and Wood Duck. In addition, there is often a contingent of Ring-necked Duck. Scan the ridges for Turkey Vulture, Osprey, Red-tailed, Broad-winged and Sharp-shinned Hawks, and Northern Raven (nesting on ledges nearby). Later during May there may be shorebirds around the remnants of the ponds and rain pools in the fields.

Proceed north on Route 5 for about 5.5 miles. Turn right onto a narrow unpaved and sometimes muddy road at the north end of the small village of Weathersfield Bow. The road traverses a fine mix of large fields, some fallow, others cultivated, and riparian woodlots. This area has not been birded with any regularity but holds the promise of fine observing. The fields and hedgerows should be especially good in autumn for migratory Horned Lark, Water Pipit, and sparrows. During April, May, and September the riparian woods could be good for small migratory landbirds. The road terminates along the bend of the Connecticut River from which the village receives its name. The river should contain ducks in fair numbers from time to time during the migratory periods.

Return to Route 5 and turn right, continuing
northward to the village of Ascutney. Cross Route
131 at the traffic light and proceed north for 1.25
miles. Bear left on the road marked by a sign indicating Ascutney State Park. The entrance to the
park is a little over a mile further. Mt. Ascutney
is a large granite monadnock covered with northern
hardwood and coniferous forest. There are three
fine hiking trails up the mountain from the south,
north, and east approaches, and the park itself
features a fine graded roadway to the South Peak
with an easy hike to the summit from the parking lot
at its terminus. The park offers camping with pay
showers in season. If one cannot find a site here,
camping sites are also provided at Wilgus State Park
south of Ascutney village. Mt. Ascutney is ideal
for observing the birdlife of the mountains of Vermont with little effort.

The best way to observe the birdlife of the
mountain is by hiking up one of the three trails
maintained by the Ascutney Trails Association. For
a comprehensive guide to the mountain's trail system as well as fine references to the history of the
mountain, write the Ascutney Trails Association at
Windsor, Vermont, for the guidebook which this organization publishes. If the observer is in a less
athletic mood, one may use the toll road. (A state
park day use fee is charged.) The road begins at
the state park headquarters at the southeastern foot
of the mountain. The road proceeds steeply through
northern hardwood forest. After about 2 miles there
is a large parking area for a picnic area and observation point. The forest along the road and around
the picnic area harbor Barred Owl, Yellow-bellied
Sapsucker, Pileated Woodpecker, Least Flycatcher,
Eastern Pewee, Red-breasted Nuthatch, Brown Creeper, Winter Wren, Wood and Hermit Thrushes, Veery,
Solitary and Red-eyed Vireos, Black-and-white,
Yellow-rumped, Black-throated Blue, Black-throated
Green, Blackburnian and Canada Warblers, Ovenbird,
American Redstart, Scarlet Tanager, Rose-breasted

Grosbeak, Northern Junco, and White-throated Sparrow.
Continue up the mountain for another 1.5 miles to
the next observation point. From here the observer
has a broad view of the Connecticut River Valley and
New Hampshire. Scan for hawks, Turkey Vulture, and
Northern Raven. Nesting landbirds include Nashville, Magnolia, Yellow-rumped and Canada Warblers,
Northern Junco, and White-throated Sparrow. Proceed to the summit lot. Park and hike to the top
from here. It is about .75 of a mile to the North
Peak from the lot. The birds along the lower trail
are similar to those mentioned for the lower picnic
area. Around the summit the forest is dominated by
Red Spruce and Balsam Fir. Birds to be seen there
during summer include Winter Wren, Swainson's Thrush,
Golden-crowned Kinglet, Magnolia and Blackpoll Warblers.

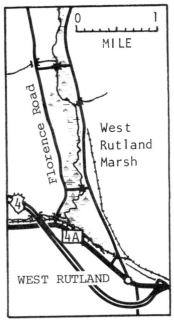

5. WEST RUTLAND

Season Key: Spring ***
               Summer **
               Autumn **

Recommended Time to Visit:
     April 15 - October 15

     North of the town of
West Rutland lies one of the
best and the most accessible
cattail and sedge marshes
in the state, and far and
away the best in southern
Vermont. To reach the West
Rutland Marsh enter West
Rutland on U.S. Route 4.
Get off Route 4 and proceed
into town on Route 4A. Turn
right at the traffic light at the center of the village and drive north on Marble Street for 1.25 miles.
Turn left onto the causeway crossing the marsh.

28

Birds that may be seen or heard from the causeway
include American Bittern, Least Bittern, American
Black Duck, Virginia Rail, Sora, Common Gallinule,
Marsh Wren, and Swamp Sparrow. In late April, May,
and June the American Bittern is usually easy to see
and hear at the marsh, with counts of four or five
not uncommon. The diminutive Least Bittern is much
more difficult to see, but with luck an observer may
observe two or three in an hour's time. The usual
sighting involves catching a glimpse of a bird in
the air as it skims low over the cattails for dis-
tances of 60 to 300 feet. The rails are best found
with the aid of tapes. By far the commoner of the
two smaller species is the Virginia Rail. The Sora
seems to prefer the sedgy portions of the marsh to
those dominated by cattails. Check the high ridge
to the west for soaring Turkey Vultures, hawks, and
Northern Raven.

Continuing across the causeway, turn right at
its west end and proceed north on the Florence road.
The woodlands along this road harbor Great Crested
Flycatcher, Eastern Peewee, Winter Wren (uncommon),
Wood Thrush, Veery, Yellow-throated, Solitary and
Warbling Vireos, Black-and-white and Canada Warblers,
Ovenbird, Northern Oriole, Scarlet Tanager, and Rose-
breasted Grosbeak. After about 1.5 miles turn right
onto a road which re-crosses the Castleton River.
Proceed to a narrow unpaved road and park out of the
way of traffic. Walk back across the river, check-
ing the fields on the west bank and the alders along
the river. Birds in this area include Common Snipe
(winnowing overhead), Black-billed Cuckoo, Alder,
Willow and Least Flycatchers, Cedar Waxwing, Warbling Vireo, Yellow and Chestnut-sided Warblers,
Bobolink, Eastern Meadowlark, Savannah and Swamp
Sparrows. Sedge Wren has nested in the wet portions
of the hayfield but its occurrence has been erratic.

For more chances to observe these birds and
many of those mentioned for the Florence road, proceed north up the unpaved road, stopping periodic-

American Bittern

MARTIN

ally to look for birds until you arrive at a right
hand fork. Park out of the way here as it is not
wise to drive further. The road narrows and conditions may vary from barely passable to horrendous.
Nonetheless, if one walks onward there is good birding to be had; species seen in this area include
Blue-grey Gnatcatcher and Golden-winged Warbler.
Retrace your steps to the pavement and continue in a
straight direction, which returns you to West Rutland. Check the open water, marshy areas, and thickets along the edge of the marsh for American Bittern,
Green Heron, Common Gallinule, and Willow Flycatcher.

Get onto the west bound lane of Route 4 upon
your return to West Rutland. Get off at the first
roadside rest area, known locally as Golden-winged
Pull-off. The hillside above the rest area is an
overgrown pasture covered with alder, hawthorn, and
briars. Birds seen on this hillside include Yellow-
billed Cuckoo, Ruby-throated Hummingbird, Brown
Thrasher, Golden-winged Warbler, Indigo Bunting, and
Field Sparrow. The initial appearance of a male
Blue-winged Warbler in May, 1980, is perhaps a por-
tent of things to come for this small (four to five
pair) Golden-winged Warbler colony.

6. NORTHWESTERN RUTLAND COUNTY

Season Key: Spring **
               Summer **
               Autumn **

Recommended Time to Visit: March 15 - November 15

One of the more unusual environments in the state may be found in the northwestern portions of Rutland County. This area is where the Taconic Mountains and the Champlain Lowlands meet and meld almost imperceptibly into each other. Lying in pockets in the northern Taconics are at least 36 lakes and ponds. The largest of these is Lake Bomoseen, over seven miles long and over a mile wide at its broadest. East of Lake Bomoseen in Pittsford and West Rutland, the Taconics are fairly high and heavily forested. The highest named mountains are Grandpa Knob (1,976 feet) and Biddie Knob (2,008 feet); several unnamed peaks match or exceed these elevations. Birds nesting in these hills are typical of the mixed woodlands of the Green Mountains and central Vermont. West of Bomoseen the hills are lower; the higher summits barely clear 1,000 feet. This area is more heavily agricultural, with more varied habitat. Some bird species typical of most Vermont hill country are rare or absent here (e.g. Magnolia Warbler). This is made up for by the relatively higher numbers of such uncommon or local species as Yellow-billed Cuckoo, Yellow-throated Vireo, and Golden-winged Warbler. Further west the hills become even lower and the intensiveness of farming increases. The land along Lake Champlain itself is very wet with both marshes and swamps represented.

In spite of the intriguing qualities of this area, it has only recently been explored by birders. Even at present, the region holds much potential. Due to the scattered nature of the most attractive locations, each area will be considered separately.

The most heavily birded site has been Lake Bomoseen. The lake, because of its size, attracts many
diving ducks. The lake also has marshy shallows attractive to dabblers. To reach the lake, take U.S.
Route 4 west from Rutland or east from Fair Haven.
The Lake Bomoseen exit is prominently marked. Proceed north on Route 30. The lake will be seen on
the left after approximately 1.75 miles. This area
is where the lake is broadest. Under good conditions
diving ducks may be seen from this vantage including
Common Goldeneye, Bufflehead, Ring-necked Duck, and
mergansers. Ring-billed Gulls are often in evidence
during the warmer months. Two miles further on, the
lake narrows. Check for waterbirds at the public
beach on the left. Three miles further is a pull-
off at the northern end of the lake, which is shallow with marshy shores. This area is conducive to
good waterfowl migrations. The more common species
are Mallard, American Black Duck, Blue-winged and
Green-winged Teal, Wood Duck, Ring-necked Duck, Common Goldeneye, Bufflehead, Common and Hooded Merganser. Other species make occasional appearances.
The marshes attract a few breeding Mallards, American Black Ducks, Wood Ducks, American Bitterns,
Green Herons, Common Gallinules, Virginia Rails, and
Marsh Wrens. Check the waters at the north end
whenever there is a reasonable opportunity. Continue
on Route 30 and take the first left about .75 of a
mile north of the lake. Continue on this road for
1.75 miles, checking the two ponds on the left (Austin and Roach) en route. Bear left onto a southbound road. There are three more small ponds next
to or near this road including Half Moon Pond, the
site of a state park of the same name. After Memorial Day the park offers both campsites and lean-tos.
Lake Bomoseen State Park may be reached by continuing south for two more miles from Half Moon Pond
State Park. The park lies between Glen Lake and
Lake Bomoseen and offers tent and trailer sites and
a naturalist program in season. Glen Lake should be
worth checking during migration. By continuing
south on this road one may scan the open waters of

the south end of Bomoseen on the left when the op-
portunity arises. The road eventually passes under
Route 4 and joins Route 4A about 1.5 miles west of
Fair Haven.

Another lake worth checking in this area is
Lake Hortonia, whicn is about four miles north of
Lake Bomoseen on Route 30. The best method of viewing this lake is to take Route 141 west along the
northern shore. A good spot to check is the vicinity of the state fishing access which borders an attractive small marsh harboring a few nesting American Black Ducks, Wood Ducks, Virginia Rails, and
Swamp Sparrows. The birder interested in exploring
new territory might be rewarded by an interesting
sighting at Sunset and Sunrise Lakes which lie to
the west of Lake Hortonia in Benson (consult maps
for exact location).

Brushy pasture land in the hill country west of
Lake Bomoseen supports the following breeding species: American Kestrel, Black-billed and Yellow-
billed Cuckoos, Whip-poor-will, Ruby-throated Hummingbird, Eastern Kingbird, Willow Flycatcher, House
Wren, Brown Thrasher, Grey Catbird, Eastern Bluebird
(local), Cedar Waxwing, Yellow-throated and Warbling
Vireos, Golden-winged (uncommon), Yellow and Chestnut-sided Warblers, Northern Cardinal, Indigo Bunting, American Goldfinch, Vesper, Chipping, Field,
White-throated and Song Sparrows.

Another area in northwestern Rutland County
which is well worth a visit is West Haven. West
Haven may be reached by proceeding north on Route
22A from Fair Haven. After about three miles turn
left onto Main Road. Main Road, as its name indicates, is the major paved road in the township of
West Haven. The woodlands and pastures of this rolling countryside are worthy of exploration. The
birdlife of the pastureland is similar to that noted
for the hills west of Bomoseen. Woodland species
include Ruffed Grouse, Common Screech Owl, Great

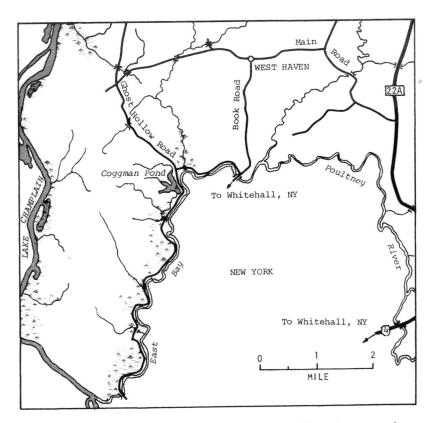

Crested Flycatcher, Eastern Pewee, White-breasted
Nuthatch, Wood Thrush, Veery, Red-eyed Vireo, Black-
and-white Warbler, Ovenbird, American Redstart, Scarlet Tanager, and Rose-breasted Grosbeak. Hay fields
harbor Upland Sandpiper (a few), Bobolink, Eastern
Meadowlark, and Savannah Sparrow. Other species
which have nested near Main Road are Red-headed
Woodpecker and Long-eared Owl.

At the village of West Haven turn south onto
Book Road. At two miles one reaches the bridge over
East Bay to Whitehall, New York. Turn right onto
the narrow, unpaved road along the north shore of
East Bay. After 1.25 miles an intersection and a
pond will appear. At Coggman Pond check the open
water during migration for waterbirds. Bear left or
walk onto the narrow, unpaved, unnamed road which
continues to follow East Bay for over five miles.

Be forewarned that this road is best traveled on
foot or with four-wheel drive. At the best of times
this road is bumpy and may have wet or downright
nasty spots. However, the habitat is fascinating
and speaks of rare sightings in future years. The
area is one of extensive swampland, hayfields,
marshes, ponds, and rich riparian woodland. The major feature of the avifauna during breeding season is
the large population of Blue-grey Gnatcatchers, far
and away the largest in the state. Counts of up to
fifteen have been achieved here, and higher counts
should be possible. Other species breeding along
East Bay include Green Heron, American Bittern,
American Black Duck, Mallard, Wood Duck, Red-tailed
Hawk, American Kestrel, Spotted Sandpiper, Yellow-
billed and Black-billed Cuckoos, Common Screech Owl,
Belted Kingfisher, Great Crested Flycatcher, Eastern
Pewee, Rough-winged Swallow, Brown Creeper, Marsh
Wren, Yellow-throated and Warbling Vireos, Bobolink,
Eastern Meadowlark, Northern Oriole, Indigo Bunting,
Savannah, Field and Swamp Sparrows.

A good method of returning to West Haven village is to turn north at Coggman Pond and proceed on
the Ghost Hollow Road which traverses some fine
woodlots and reaches Main Road after about two miles.
Turn right onto Main Road; West Haven is reached after 2.5 miles. Route 22A is 2.5 miles beyond the
village. As with prior sections of Main Road, the
countryside between the village and Ghost Hollow
Road is well worth birding.

To the north in Orwell lie the East Creek
Marshes, virtually unbirded and well worth a check.
To reach this area, continue north on Route 22A
through the town of Benson. At 2.75 miles north of
the junction with Route 141, just prior to the town
line, take a left. After .6 of a mile turn right.
This road parallels the South Fork of East Creek and
intersects with Route 73A west of Orwell village.
The land surrounding the creek is largely owned by
the state as a waterfowl area. The marshes along

the creek should support typical marsh birds including rails and bitterns and have a good waterfowl migration in spring and autumn. North of Route 73A East Creek meanders to Lake Champlain. The creek is surrounded by an extensive shallow marsh featuring large beds of Narrow-leaved Cattail. The best method of exploring this difficult-of-access region is via canoe.

7. KILLINGTON PEAK REGION

Season Key: Spring **
              Summer ***
              Autumn **

Recommended Time to Visit: April 30 - October 31

Killington Peak is in the Green Mountain Range and is the second highest mountain in the state at 4,241 feet above sea level. The peak is at the center of one of the busiest winter playgrounds in North America. However, winter is not an opportune time for the visiting birder. Weather in the mountains is forbidding from November to March; only a handful of birds remain to face the fury of montane storms. With the arrival of warmer conditions, the mountains possess abundant (and oft times noisome) insect life which attracts a wide variety of breeding birds. The area hosts 104 breeding species including 18 warblers, 8 flycatchers, and 6 thrushes, featuring Grey-cheeked.

The mountain itself and its satellite peaks, Pico and Shrewsbury, are the focus of birding interest, but several outlying areas are also worthwhile for the enterprising field observer. A good place to begin one's explorations is at Sherburne Center (Killington post office), 13 miles east of Rutland on U.S. Route 4. Turn north off Route 4 onto the River Road which follows the Ottauquechee River. Less than a half mile farther, Sherburne Marsh will

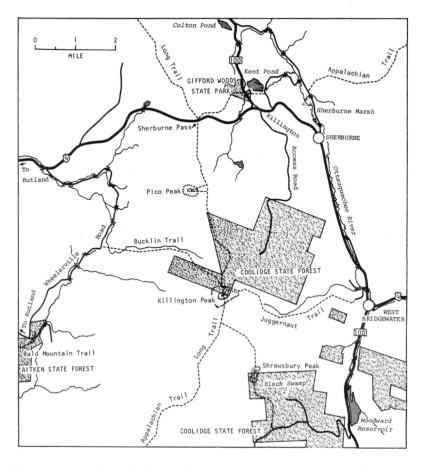

be seen on the left. The marsh is a region of extensive beaver activity, with pools overgrown with
sedges and cattails. The older pools have become
filled in with alders and other swamp vegetation.
The swamp and marsh vegetation are at their best for
the next mile of the River Road. Species which
breed in and near the marsh include American Bittern
(uncommon), American Black Duck, American Kestrel,
Killdeer, American Woodcock, Common Snipe, Black-
billed Cuckoo, Belted Kingfisher, Eastern Kingbird,
Great Crested Flycatcher, Alder Flycatcher, Tree
Swallow, White-breasted Nuthatch, Grey Catbird,
Veery, Cedar Waxwing, Warbling Vireo, Yellow, Chestnut-sided and Canada Warblers, Northern Waterthrush,

Common Yellowthroat, Red-winged Blackbird, Northern Oriole, Rose-breasted Grosbeak, Indigo Bunting, American Goldfinch, White-throated, Swamp and Song Sparrows.

At 1.5 miles from Route 4, turn left and cross the Ottauquechee and proceed 1.75 miles through mixed woodlands to Kent Pond. The road continues along the earthen dam which creates this medium size pond. During spring and fall migration, Common Loons can often be found serenely patrolling the surface of the pond. Other migratory waterfowl and the occasional shorebird, gull or cormorant make the pond a worthwhile stop for the birder. The wet Balsam Fir wood on the east side of the dam often has interesting transients in spring and harbors nesting Red-breasted Nuthatch, Wood Thrush, Veery, Solitary Vireo, Magnolia and Yellow-rumped Warblers.

Continue on; after about a half mile the road rejoins Route 4. Turn right onto Route 4 and proceed to the junction with state Route 100 north. Turn onto Route 100, driving for another half mile to the entrance to Gifford Woods State Park on the left. This small park offers camping and picnicking and features the most accessible remaining virgin northern hardwoods in the state. Birds nesting among the huge Yellow Birches, Sugar Maples, beeches, and hemlocks are Least Flycatcher, Eastern Pewee, White-breasted Nuthatch, Brown Creeper, Wood and Hermit Thrush, Veery, Solitary and Red-eyed Vireos, Northern Parula (one or two pair), Black-throated Blue, Black-throated Green, and Blackburnian Warblers, Ovenbird, American Redstart, Scarlet Tanager, Northern Junco, and White-throated Sparrow.

Approximately two miles farther along on Route 100 on the left is the Colton Pond Fishing Access. Colton Pond is an attractive, small mountain pond with mountains rising above its western shore and pine woodlands and overgrown beaver meadows on the east. The pond is worth a check during migration

38

for waterbirds and transient landbirds and hosts
breeding Spotted Sandpiper, Belted Kingfisher,
Great Horned Owl, Red-breasted Nuthatch, Brown
Creeper, Wood and Hermit Thrushes, Cedar Waxwing,
Solitary Vireo, Black-and-white, Yellow-rumped,
Blackburnian and Chestnut-sided Warblers, Purple
Finch, White-throated and Swamp Sparrows.

Return to U.S. Route 4; proceed onto the Killington Access Road just east of Route 100 north.
The woodlots along this road harbor typical woodland
birds. The road is also studded with the inevitable
ski area resort inns and bars. The area around the
base lodge at the end often has a pair of Olive-sided
Flycatchers. Barn Swallows nest in every available
cranny of this edifice. The more overgrown side
trails at the base of the ski "hill" have a few
nesting Canada and Mourning Warblers and Indigo Buntings. The summit of Killington Peak may be reached
by hiking up the ski trails, but this is not recommended as the trails are very steep and strenuous.
The birder would be far better served by the hiking
trails mentioned in later portions of this section.

Two of these trails (the Long Trail and the
Bucklin Trail) are reached by returning to Route 4
and proceeding west up Sherburne Pass. At the crest
of the pass, at 2,150 feet above sea level, the Long
Trail crosses U.S. Route 4. To reach Killington
Peak via Pico Peak (3,957 feet) take the trail south
from Route 4. At 2.1 miles one reaches the north
end of the loop trail to the summit of Pico. The
summit is reached after a relatively steep climb of
.4 of a mile. Birds to be looked for in the hard-
woods below 3,000 feet include Broad-winged Hawk,
Ruffed Grouse, Barred Owl, Yellow-bellied Sapsucker,
Least Flycatcher, Eastern Pewee, White-breasted
Nuthatch, Winter Wren, Wood and Hermit Thrushes,
Veery, Solitary and Red-eyed Vireos, Black-throated
Blue, Black-throated Green, Blackburnian and Canada
Warblers, Ovenbird, American Redstart, Scarlet Tana-
ger, and Rose-breasted Grosbeak. Mourning and Nash-

Grey-cheeked Thrush

N
MARTIN

ville Warblers should be looked for in brushy clearings. Above 3,000 feet, especially in the thick
coniferous growth on the Pico spur trail, such species as Yellow-bellied Flycatcher, Red-breasted Nuthatch, Brown Creeper, Winter Wren, Swainson's and
Grey-cheeked Thrushes, Golden-crowned Kinglet, Yellow-rumped, Magnolia and Blackpoll Warblers, Northern Junco, and White-throated Sparrow breed. If the
observer wishes to continue to Killington with its
larger population of Grey-cheeked Thrushes, the
Cooper Lodge is about three miles beyond the Pico
Camp at the south end of the Pico Loop. A steep ascent of about .2 of a mile gives access to the summit of Killington from Cooper Lodge. An overnight
at Cooper Lodge or Pico Camp is recommended as the
evening and dawn chorus of thrushes is quite impressive. If the observer chooses not to use this
route, the forest in the pass has several trails
running through it which offer many of the birds indicated for the initial stages of the Long Trail to
Pico and Killington.

Another fine birding area may be reached by
continuing on Route 4 west for about 4.4 miles,
turning left onto Wheelerville Road. This road
passes through fine hardwood forests with occasional
stands of conifers offering a wide range of woodland
birds during migration and the breeding season. After four miles the parking space for the Bucklin
Trail will be seen just before a sharp right turn in

the road. This trail ascends to Cooper Lodge covering 3.4 miles of montane forest. Three miles further the Wheelerville Road joins the Notch Road. Taking a left onto the Notch Road and descending a short hill brings you to the former Tamarack Notch Girl Scout Camp. The Bald Mountain Trail, which follows a gradual path leading to the summit of the 2,090 foot peak in Aitken State Forest, originates here. The trail, marked by blue blazes, is reached by following the logging road located on the right just before the Notch Road crosses a (sometimes dry) brook near the camp gate. The trail turns right, off the logging road, after about .1 of a mile. The woodlands on the north slopes are typical northern hardwoods consisting of Eastern Hemlock, Yellow Birch, Beech and Sugar Maple; the south slopes are covered with oak, pine, and hickory. Hermit Thrushes, Black-throated Blue Warblers, and Northern Juncos are common here. Trails proceed from the summit to the south slopes where several clearings yield excellent vistas of the southern Green Mountains, Taconics, and the Valley of Vermont. The best view may be had from Red Rocks Lookout. Some good hawk flights have been seen from these ledges. Turkey Vultures are often seen about the ledges in spring, summer, and fall. The Notch Road will return you to the eastern edge of Rutland city if followed back past the Wheelerville Road and down the hill.

Another worthy area to visit is Plymouth, which is reached from Sherburne Center by proceeding east on Route 4 to the village of West Bridgewater and the junction with Route 100 south. On the way, note the Killington Gondola, which conveys tourists to the summit of Killington Peak for a price. This offers the path of least resistance to the summit for those not wishing to include an arduous hike in their vacation. However, take note that an overnight at Cooper Lodge, in spite of its rustic qualities, is necessary if observers wish to hear Grey-cheeked Thrushes in full voice. The small chapel on

the River Road across the narrow valley has a small
colony of Cliff Swallows.

The left branch of a side road .2 of a mile west
of the junction of Routes 4 and 100 in West Bridge-
water leads to the head of the Juggernaut Trail.
This is yet another trail to the Cooper Lodge and
offers birds similar to those along the Long Trail.
It reaches the lodge after a 4.5 mile hike. More
detailed descriptions of the side trails and the
Long Trail may be had from the Green Mountain Club's
Guide Book of the Long Trail. Two miles south of
West Bridgewater is Woodward Reservoir (pronounced
Wood-dard). As with Kent Pond, interesting migratory waterbirds are often seen here; noteworthy are
Common Loons, Common Goldeneye, and mergansers.
Take a right .2 of a mile beyond the south end of
the reservoir onto an unpaved state forest highway
which climbs steeply into the Shrewsbury section of
the Calvin Coolidge State Forest. After approxi-
mately 2 miles, turn right onto a yellow-gated road;
the gate is usually open. After a short drive or
walk, the road crosses the outlet stream of Black
Swamp which will be on the right. Black Swamp is a
Red Spruce bog in the shadow of Shrewsbury Peak.
The swamp has a wide variety of boreal bird species
breeding in and around it including Yellow-bellied
Flycatcher, Red-breasted Nuthatch, Winter Wren,
Hermit and Swainson's Thrushes, Ruby-crowned Kinglet
(uncommon), Nashville, Magnolia, Blackburnian,
Blackpoll and Canada Warblers, Rusty Blackbird (a
few), Northern Junco, and White-throated Sparrow.
Returning to the original state forest highway, one
may continue and take the next right to the head of
the Shrewsbury Peak Trail which leads to the summit
of this imposing 3,720 foot mountain after a 1.8
mile climb. The blue-blazed trail begins behind the
old log Northam picnic shelter. The birds on the
summit are similar to those of Killington and Pico
Peaks. The trail continues another 2 miles to the
Long Trail, and about 1 mile to the north lies
Cooper Lodge.

8. WOODSTOCK

Season Key: Spring **
              Summer **
              Autumn **
              Winter *

Recommended Time to Visit: Year Round
                             Best from April 1 -
                             October 31

Woodstock is a small town in the east central portion of the state in the valley of the Ottauquechee River. Its virtues as a typical Vermont postcard town are well known. There are several areas around Woodstock which allow the visiting birder to experience the typical birds of this section of the state. The best way to approach Woodstock is via U.S. Route 4 either from Rutland or White River Junction.

East of town lies the floodplain of the Ottauquechee River. To reach this area, turn downhill off Route 4 east of town at the sign indicating the local office of the Central Vermont Public Service Corporation. Proceed past the office and park next to the small power sub-station. There are several large fields here, some cultivated for corn and others for hay. Across the fields, about a quarter of a mile away, are two small wooded oxbows; beyond them lies the river. This area is best during migration, but expected nesting species would be Mourning Dove, Belted Kingfisher, Grey Catbird, Common Yellowthroat, Bobolink, Eastern Meadowlark, and Northern Cardinal. The floodplain could harbor almost anything during migration, but the specialties are sparrows and raptors. Sparrows include Savannah, Vesper, Chipping, Field, American Tree, White-throated, White-crowned, Fox, Swamp, Lincoln's, Song, and Northern Junco. The raptors most often seen are Sharp-shinned, Red-tailed and Broad-winged Hawks, Osprey, and American Kestrel; but Northern Goshawk,

Rough-legged Hawk, and Northern Shrike have also been
found here. A pair of Great Horned Owls hunt the
fields at night and can sometimes be heard calling in
the large willows along the river. In late October
and early November there may be Horned Lark, Water
Pipit, Snow Bunting, and Lapland Longspur. Sparrows,
pipits, larks, Snow Buntings, and longspur may also
be searched for in the fields near the former Mt.
Tom Ski Area on Route 12 north from Woodstock and
along the Barnard Stage Road, which leaves Route 12
across from the ski area. Flocks of Eastern Blue-
birds may be encountered in the fall along the Stage
Road also.

     To reach the hiking trails on Mt. Tom, cross
the covered bridge near the Green and take a left onto
Mountain Avenue to Faulkner and French Memorial Parks;
the entrance to the parks is well marked. There are
several fine graded trails with switchbacks ascending to the summit of Mt. Tom (actually a hill, 1,340
feet in elevation). Most of the typical breeding
birds of the northern hardwood forests of Vermont
can be seen here including Ruffed Grouse, Pileated
Woodpecker, Yellow-bellied Sapsucker, Least and
Great Crested Flycatchers, Eastern Pewee, Brown
Creeper, Wood and Hermit Thrushes, Solitary and Red-
eyed Vireos, Black-and-white, Yellow-rumped, Black-
throated Blue, Black-throated Green, and Blackburnian Warblers, Scarlet Tanager, Rose-breasted Grosbeak, and Northern Junco. A pair of Northern Ravens
has been in residence on Mt. Tom for the last few
years.

     Return to Route 4 and continue to the west end
of the Green; take Church Hill Road which passes to
the left of the stone St. James Episcopal Church
and proceeds steeply upward. At 1.6 miles, just before the crest of the hill, the headquarters of the
Vermont Institute of Natural Science will appear on
your right. This organization, incorporated in 1972,
has become one of the most important conservation
agencies in the state. The Institute is instrumental

in environmental education and biological research throughout Vermont. Among its activities related to birds are sponsoring field trips and the annual Vermont Bird Conference (held in June each year), administering the state Breeding Bird Atlas Project, publishing the quarterly <u>Records of Vermont Birds</u>, maintaining a Rare Bird Alert (802/457-2779), and bird banding. The headquarters houses a fine natural history library with texts and journals on ornithological subjects. Much of the Institute's banding activities take place on the adjacent Bragdon Nature Preserve. To view banding here one must contact the Institute and arrange a demonstration. (There are at least two public demonstrations each year.) However, one may visit the preserve and bird without special arrangements. Many of the birds mentioned in the section on Mt. Tom breed here also. A birder will also likely encounter Brown Thrasher, Eastern Bluebird, Warbling Vireo, Nashville, Magnolia and Chestnut-sided Warblers, Rufous-sided Towhee, and Field Sparrow. The staff of VINS keeps track of the birds seen on the preserve (A list of 144 species had been compiled by November 1981.) and would appreciate observers informing a staff person of interesting sightings. Some of the more interesting species on the present list include Black-crowned Night Heron, Rough-legged Hawk, Saw-whet Owl, Blue-grey Gnatcatcher, Yellow-breasted Chat, and Connecticut Warbler.

9. LAKES MOREY AND FAIRLEE

Season Key: Spring **
              Summer *
              Autumn ***

Recommended Time to Visit: April 15 - May 10
                             October 1 - November 30

Lakes Morey and Fairlee are two fairly large lakes (2 and 2.25 miles long, respectively) in eastern Orange County which occupy glacially carved valleys just west of the Connecticut River. During spring and fall, these bodies host good, sometimes excellent, numbers of migratory waterbirds. The presence of these lakes in the Connecticut Valley may explain the good migrations that occur on them, but a more likely explanation might be that Morey and Fairlee have been blessed with good coverage over the years. The autumn migration is generally the better, as spring flights tend to be more erratic with smaller numbers of most species.

During migration, a wide variety of waterfowl and other waterbirds has been seen. Among the most numerous have been Common Loon, Mallard, American Black Duck, Wood Duck (north end of Lake Fairlee), Common Goldeneye, Bufflehead, Hooded and Common Mergansers, and Herring Gull. Other species of regular occurrence in much smaller numbers have been Pied-billed, Horned and Red-necked Grebes, Ring-necked Duck, Greater and Lesser Scaup, all three scoters, Oldsquaw, American Coot (at south end of Morey with domestic ducks), and Ring-billed Gull.

Summer is not the best of times to visit the lakes because both lakes have many camps and are usually overrun with motorized boat traffic. If an observer chances to visit in summer, he or she should look for the one to two pair of Northern Parula which nest at the north end of Lake Morey beyond the Bonnie Oaks resort. Pine Warblers nest in the tall White Pines on the east shore of Morey and at the southern end of Lake Fairlee. The hills surrounding the lakes are occupied by the typical breeding birds of the mixed woodlands of east central Vermont. These include Broad-winged Hawk, Ruffed Grouse, Barred Owl, Black-billed Cuckoo, Whip-poor-will (woodlots near the lakes), Pileated Woodpecker, Yellow-bellied Sapsucker, Great Crested Flycatcher, Least Flycatcher, Eastern Pewee, Brown Creeper, Winter Wren, Wood and Hermit Thrushes, Veery, Golden-crowned Kinglet (in hemlock, fir, and spruce stands),

Solitary and Red-eyed Vireos, Black-and-white, Magnolia, Black-throated Blue, Yellow-rumped, Black-throated Green, Blackburnian and Canada Warblers, Ovenbird, American Redstart, Scarlet Tanager, Rose-breasted Grosbeak, Northern Junco, and White-throated Sparrow. A few Louisiana Waterthrushes breed along the streams which course into the lakes.

A suggested method of viewing the lakes during migration is to go up the east side of Lake Morey on the East Shore Road which commences at the southeast corner of the lake just west of the Fairlee exit off Interstate 91. The first good access for viewing the lake is at a small pull-out at the north end just beyond the Bonnie Oaks resort complex. Proceed from here to an opening on the west shore which offers a commanding view of the central portion of the lake. The state fishing access on the west shore offers another fine viewpoint.

From Lake Morey, the best method of proceeding to Lake Fairlee is to drive south from Fairlee village on Route 5 to the small village of Ely. Turn right at Ely onto state Route 113. Lake Fairlee will be seen on the left after about two miles. Stop to scan the small marsh at the north end; this is the best spot on the tour for Wood Duck, and there is sometimes a Great Blue Heron here. The best view of the lake is from the state fishing access on the north shore adjacent to the mouth of Middle Brook. To return to Interstate 91 continue on Route 113, turning left onto Route 113A at the village of Post Mills. Route 91 is reached after 5 miles on Route 113A east.

Common Loon

10. BARRE-MONTPELIER AREA

Season Key: Spring ***
             Summer **
             Autumn ***
             Winter *

The state capital and the capital of Vermont's granite industry lie adjacent to each other in the valley of the Winooski River. The hills around these two cities are covered with northern hardwood forest, which gives way to Red Spruce and Balsam Fir on the higher elevations and in cool pockets. There are many lakes and ponds in the glacially carved valleys of the hills above the Winooski Valley. This array of habitats is in large measure responsible for the vicinity of Barre and Montpelier being considered one of the better places to bird in central Vermont.

Within the city of Montpelier, there is a good locality for viewing spring and autumn migrations. This is Hubbard Park, owned and maintained by the city. The park lies on an 860 foot hill between State, Elm, and Terrace Streets. The park features ornamental plantings of both deciduous and coniferous trees and shrubs. During migration, especially in spring when transients are in full voice, the park is worth a visit for a good mixture of migratory flycatchers, thrushes, vireos, and warblers. Starting from the state capitol building one may reach the park by proceeding west on State Street. At Bailey Avenue, turn right and then turn left onto Terrace Street. At about a third of a mile, turn right onto Hubbard Park Drive which proceeds uphill to the park.

A good location for waterbirds, which, however, offers only limited access, is Berlin Pond. To reach Berlin Pond, get on Interstate 89 at Exit 8 in Montpelier and proceed on the southbound lane to Exit 7. Get off the interstate here and continue toward Barre. Turn right at the traffic lights and take the next right after that. After about one quarter of a mile turn left and proceed under Interstate 89. After the underpass Berlin Pond, the reservoir for the city of Montpelier, will be on the left. The north end of the pond is sinuous and is bordered by alders and some cattails. Much of this portion of the pond may be seen from the road. Migratory waterbirds of many species have been seen here. A telescope is useful at this location. In April of 1980 a pair of Whistling Swans was seen here, indicating the potential of this spot. Unfortunately, much of the pond's shoreline is far from the road and off limits, as it is a protected watershed.

Another reservoir in the area which has proved an excellent area for birding is Thurman W. Dix Reservoir, owned by the Barre Water Department. To reach this body of water, return to the traffic lights and turn right. At about one mile, take Route 62 into Barre. Upon reaching the traffic lights at Route 302 turn right and take Route 302 east toward East Barre. Just east of this village take the first left hand turn. At about 2.25 miles the reservoir will be seen at left. Thurman W. Dix Reservoir is about .75 of a mile long and over a quarter of a mile wide. The reservoir is best during migration when a wide variety of waterbirds utilizes it as a resting place. Species seen here include Common Loon, Horned, Red-necked and Pied-billed Grebes, Great Blue and Green Herons, Canada Goose, Mallard, American Black Duck, both teal, Ring-necked Duck, Common Goldeneye, Bufflehead, Common, Red-breasted and Hooded Mergansers. Shorebirds may be numerous in late summer during dry years; sightings have included such rarities as Northern and Wilson's Phalaropes. One observer has noted 191 species of birds in twenty years of birding at the reservoir. As with Berlin Pond, the shoreline of the reservoir is off limits as it is a public water supply. However, the observer can quite satisfactorily view the water from the road skirting the reservoir.

From Thurman W. Dix Reservoir the birder may reach Plainfield, about six miles away, by proceeding north on the right hand fork at the northwestern corner of the reservoir. At Plainfield, turn right onto U.S. Route 2. At eight miles, a mile beyond the village of Marshfield, turn onto the Groton/ Marshfield State Highway to the boundary of Groton State Forest, five miles distant. This state forest is the largest in the state's system of parks and forests Encompassing 25,625 acres, it comprises nearly 16 percent of the acreage in the system. Embraced within its boundaries are mountains, hills, bogs, beaver meadows, and six lakes and ponds. The largest body of water within the forest is Lake Groton, over 2.5 miles long and .4 of a mile wide at its broadest. The highest point in the park is an unnamed peak above Pigeon Pond which stands 2,780 feet above sea level. The wide range of habitats within the forest are inhabited by a fine variety

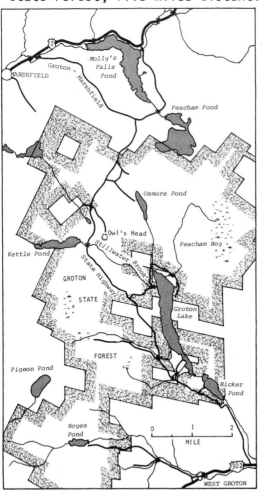

50

of breeding birds, including at least 16 species of warblers. The area is also worth a visit during migration. The Department of Forest and Parks has developed a checklist of the birds of the forest; this may be obtained by writing the department in Montpelier, Vermont, 05602. There are good camping facilities in the state forest at four locations, with pay showers, campsites, lean-tos, boat rentals, and swimming beaches.

From the northern approach, the first birding area of interest is Owl's Head, a rounded granite knoll 1,958 feet in elevation. This area may be reached by taking the third left after entering the state forest. The road climbs to a parking area with picnic facilities. The partially cleared summit is reached via a short, steep trail. The summit offers a fine view of the state forest and the surrounding towns. Birds which might be seen here include Ruffed Grouse, Yellow-bellied Sapsucker, Northern Raven, Red-breasted Nuthatch, Brown Creeper, Winter Wren, Wood, Hermit and Swainson's Thrushes, Golden-crowned Kinglet, Solitary Vireo, Magnolia, Black-throated Blue, Yellow-rumped, Black-throated Green, Blackburnian and Canada Warblers, Scarlet Tanager, Rose-breasted Grosbeak, and Northern Junco. This area has been used with limited success as a hawk lookout during migration. An added attraction during spring and autumn are flocks of geese regularly passing over.

About 1.2 miles south of the turn to Owl's Head on the right is a trail to Kettle Pond. The pond is relatively isolated and is surrounded with spruce-fir woodland. The pond is a good area for Yellow-bellied and Olive-sided Flycatchers, Northern Raven, Red-breasted Nuthatch, Brown Creeper, Winter Wren, Wood, Hermit and Swainson's Thrushes, Veery, Ruby-crowned and Golden-crowned Kinglets, Solitary and Red-eyed Vireos, Nashville, Northern Parula, Magnolia, Black-throated Blue, Yellow-rumped, Black-throated Green, Blackburnian, Mourning and Canada Warblers, North-

ern Waterthrush, Scarlet Tanager, Rose-breasted
Grosbeak, Purple Finch, Northern Junco, and White-
throated Sparrow. On the east side of the highway
the adventurous observer with a taste for explora-
tory "bushwacking" may follow Stillwater Brook, the
outlet stream of Kettle Pond, to some productive
beaver meadows, good for a similar array of species
as Kettle Pond, plus Rusty Blackbird and perhaps
Lincoln's Sparrow.

During migratory periods the larger ponds and
lakes, in particular Lake Groton, should host waterfowl including loons, grebes, and various ducks.

To visit another good area for migratory waterbirds return north on the Groton/Marshfield State
Highway. At U.S. Route 2 turn right and proceed for
1.5 miles to Molly's Falls Pond. This lake provides
worthwhile birding especially in autumn. Birds seen
here include Common Loons, grebes, scoters, Oldsquaw,
and mergansers. During late summer this pond is a
good location for sighting Solitary Sandpiper, Common Snipe, and other shorebirds.

11. THE LINCOLN RANGE

Recommended Time to Visit: May 30 - July 20

This area is the home of the Sugarbush/Mad River
Ski Area complex. The major ornithological attractions of this region are the breeding birds of the
mountains. Between Lincoln and Appalachian Gaps,
the Green Mountains is a uniformly high elevation
ridge averaging over 3,400 feet. The ridge supports
a thick, unbroken, stunted spruce-fir woodland. The
birds of the Lincoln Range are largely the same as
those of Killington Peak, Camel's Hump, and Mt. Mansfield.

Access to the Lincoln Range may be had only on
foot. Trail access is available via the Long Trail
at Lincoln and Appalachian Gaps, two well maintained

side trails on the west side of the ridge, the Jerusalem and Battell Trails, and the ski trails (not recommended) from the east side. There are overnight accommodations for backpackers on the Long Trail at three locations: the Battell Shelter just south of the summit of Mt. Abraham (4,006 feet), the Glen Ellen Lodge situated north of the summit of General Stark Mountain (3,662 feet), and the Theron Dean Shelter between Appalachian Gap and General Stark Mountain at 3,330 feet. The Glen Ellen Lodge has more space, bunking eight to ten versus six to eight for the Battell Shelter and four to six for the Theron Dean Shelter. The first two shelters are at elevations of 3,250 feet. The breeding birds of the ridge include Ruffed Grouse, Yellow-bellied Flycatcher, Northern Raven, Winter Wren, Swainson's and Grey-cheeked Thrushes, and Blackpoll Warbler.

To reach Appalachian Gap take Route 17 west at Irasville or east from its junction with Route 116 east of Bristol. The crest of the gap reaches 2,377 feet in elevation. The Long Trail proceeds south to General Stark Mountain in 2.6 miles. Mount Ellen (4,083 feet) is 2.2 miles further along. To reach Lincoln Gap from the east take the Lincoln-Warren Highway, a westbound road, at the south end of Warren on Route 100. The road reaches the gap (2,410 feet) after 4.7 miles. The Long Trail on the right proceeds north 1.8 miles to the Battell Shelter and 2.6 miles to the summit of Mount Abraham.

From the summit of Lincoln Gap, the Lincoln-Warren Highway proceeds steeply downhill for 4.7 miles into the town of Lincoln. The northern hardwood forests along the road harbor the typical birds of this habitat. Mourning Warblers have been seen during summer in brushy spots along the way down. To reach the head of the Battell Trail, turn right at the green in the village. Continue for .6 of a mile, passing a cemetery on the left. Prior to crossing Beaver Brook, turn right; proceed straight on this road for two miles to the head of the Battel Trail. The trail proceeds uphill from the right angle turn at two miles. The aspen, Grey Birch, and alder brush near the trail head has such breeding birds as Ruby-throated Hummingbird, Alder Flycatcher, Brown Thrasher, Black-and-white, Nashville and Chestnut-sided Warblers, Indigo Bunting, Rufous-sided Towhee and Field Sparrow. Beyond the trail head on the road to the left there is a clear cut which has a good nesting population of Mourning Warblers.

The Battell Trail proceeds two miles up a moderate grade to the Battell Shelter. Hiking up a side trail such as this allows a birder to sample the birdlife of the various forest types from the base of the mountain to the summit.

The Jerusalem Trail offers another route to the ridge. To reach the trail head one must turn east off Route 17, 3.25 miles east of the junction of Routes 116 and 17 or 6.2 miles west of Appalachian Gap. This road follows the valley of Baldwin Creek to a three-corners in the tiny community of Jerusalem, 1.2 miles from Route 17. At Jerusalem turn left and proceed .3 of a mile to the trail head. The trail proceeds 2.5 miles to the ridge at 3,430 feet. A tenth of a mile north of the junction with the Long Trail is the side trail to the Glen Ellen Lodge. One and eight tenths of a mile south of the junction is the summit of Mt. Ellen, tied with Camel's Hump as the third highest mountain in the state.

12. DEAD CREEK WILDLIFE MANAGEMENT AREA AND ITS ENVIRONS

Season Key: Spring ***
              Summer **
              Autumn ***
              Winter **

Recommended Time to Visit: Year Round

The marshes and farmlands of the lower Champ-

lain Valley are unique in Vermont and offer the local and visiting birder many a worthy experience
year round. Western Addison County is in the shadow
of the high peaks of New York's Adirondack Mountains.
Due to this topography, the area receives the least
rainfall in the state. However, the county is well
watered by streams flowing out of the mountains to
the east and south. On the broad plain of Lake
Champlain, these streams meander across the flat
landscape. The major stream of the region is the
Otter Creek, the longest stream in the state, rising
in Bennington County well to the south. The broad
valleys of these streams are very marshy, and one
tributary of Otter Creek, Dead Creek, has been ac-
tively managed to encourage nesting and migratory
waterfowl. Because of the combination of habitats,
the Champlain Valley in Addison County, and particularly the Dead Creek Wildlife Management Area, is
the finest region for marsh birds, waterfowl, and
wintering raptors in Vermont.

The best starting point for your explorations
is the city of Vergennes, billed by its residents
as the "smallest city in the United States". Start
at the center of town and proceed south on Route 22A.
Cross the Otter Creek in town and turn right onto
the Panton Road. Continue straight for 1.4 miles
and turn right onto the Basin Harbor Road. Proceed
for two miles until one arrives at a causeway with
Otter Creek on the right and the mouth of Dead
Creek on the left. There is a small turnout along
the road. Ducks, herons, and shorebirds are often
seen in the marshy backwater of the delta of Dead
Creek. The floodplain woodlands along the Otter
Creek contain resident Great Horned and Common
Screech Owls.

Proceed from here for another two miles and
turn left onto a road marked by a sign indicating
the way to Button Bay State Park. The park is about
a mile farther on. This fine state park, which offers picnicking and camping (with hot showers for a

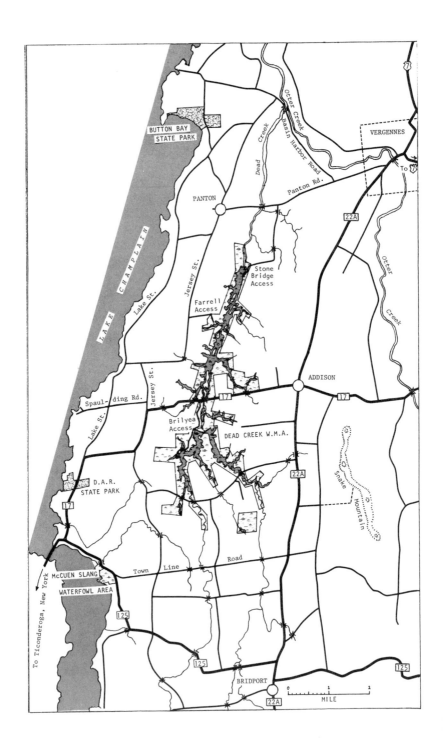

BUTTON BAY
STATE PARK

VERGENNES

To 7

Otter Creek

Basin Harbor Road

Dead Creek

Panton Rd.

PANTON

22A

Stone
Bridge
Access

Farrell
Access

Jersey St.

L A K E   C H A M P L A I N

Lake St.

Jersey St.

ADDISON

Otter Creek

Spaul—ding Rd.

17

17

Brilyea
Access

DEAD CREEK W.M.A.

Lake St.

22A

Snake Mountain

D.A.R.
STATE PARK

17

Town   Line   Road

McCUEN SLANG
WATERFOWL AREA

To Ticonderoga, New York

125

125

125

125

BRIDGPORT

22A

0   1   1
MILE

price) lies on the shores of Button Bay, named for
the peculiar button shaped concretions which have
become increasingly hard to find along the shores of
the bay. The bay is very good for migratory waterfowl of many varieties, including Common Loon, Horned
Grebe, Canada Goose, Mallard, American Black Duck,
Canvasback, both scaup, Common Goldeneye, Bufflehead,
scoters (3 species), and mergansers (3 species).
During late summer and autumn, the shoreline of Lake
Champlain often recedes, providing good shorebird
habitat. Regulars are Semipalmated Plover, Killdeer,
Least Sandpiper, Semipalmated Sandpiper, Spotted
Sandpiper, both yellowlegs, and Common Snipe. Many
other species have been seen here including such
rarities as Baird's Sandpiper and Red Phalarope.
The park grounds and the surrounding fields are good
for Red-tailed Hawk (year round), Rough-legged Hawk
(October-April), Northern Harrier (March-November),
American Kestrel (year round), and Upland Sandpiper
(April-August).

From Button Bay proceed south, bearing right and
then left, for 2.25 miles to the village of Panton
Four Corners. Turn left and proceed one mile to a
causeway and bridge crossing Dead Creek. There is a
pullout prior to the causeway on both sides. Birds
to be seen during breeding season in the marsh and
along the main channel of the creek include Great
Blue Heron, Green Heron, Black-crowned Night Heron,
American Bittern, Canada Goose, Mallard, American
Black Duck, Blue-winged Teal, Wood Duck, Northern
Harrier, Virginia Rail, Common Gallinule, Black Tern,
Belted Kingfisher, Marsh Wren, Common Yellowthroat,
and Swamp Sparrow. This area is often quite good
during migration for waders, waterfowl, and shorebirds.

Proceed straight for another .4 of a mile and
turn right onto a dirt road marked by a sign indicating a State of Vermont Fishing Access, the Stone
Bridge Access. After crossing a narrow iron bridge

over a placid stream check the fields and fencerows
for sparrows, Horned Lark (year round), Water Pipits
(April-May, September-October), Northern Harrier,
and Lesser Golden Plover. Look for the plovers in
freshly harrowed fields from late August to mid-
October. Check carefully because the birds match
the grey-brown background of the fields beautifully.
With some real luck, the observer might encounter
Loggerhead Shrike here or along the Farrell Access
Road described next. The road turns abruptly to the
right at about one and a quarter miles and continues
onward to the access. Most of the birds to be seen
at the Panton Road crossing may also be seen here.
During periods of low water the area may be good for
shorebirds.

Return to Panton Four Corners and proceed south
on Jersey Street, which parallels Dead Creek. After
about 2.75 miles take a left hand turn on a narrow
road which goes to the Farrell Access to Dead Creek.
The road to the access traverses open farmland inhabited by Bobolink, Eastern Meadowlark, Savannah
and Vesper Sparrows during breeding season. From
late May to July, Willow Flycatcher may be encountered in thickets along the stream valleys the road
crosses. The access itself is not a first rate observation point for viewing the creek but is usually
worth a check. However, it is a fine place to
launch a canoe (as are the other accesses mentioned)
for those wishing to observe the creek's wildlife
intimately and to improve their chances of seeing
Least Bittern and rails.

Return to Jersey Street and proceed south.
Continue south following the road as it right angles
toward the lake on a road called Goodrich Corners.
Turn left onto Jersey Street once again after about
a mile. Scan the large fields in this district at
any time of year. During migration one may encounter
shorebirds (Lesser Golden Plover in autumn, Pectoral
Sandpiper in spring and autumn, the Upland Sandpiper
being a summer resident and migrant), Water Pipit,

and various sparrows. During summer there are
Horned Lark, American Kestrel, Red-tailed Hawk, and
Northern Harrier, Eastern Meadowlark, and Bobolink,
Savannah and Vesper Sparrows. In winter, Red-tailed
Hawk, Rough-legged Hawk, and American Kestrel patrol
the fields, sometimes flushing large flocks of
Horned Lark and Snow Bunting. Check these flocks
for an occasional Lapland Longspur. Common Redpoll
are sometimes also present.

One mile south of the left turn, turn right and
proceed toward Lake Champlain on Spaulding Road. Continue straight, crossing Lake Street at .9 of a mile,
bear right at the fork at 1.5 miles, and drive to the
end of a narrow road to the Tri-town Water District
treatment facility. This area is particularly good
for viewing migrant waterbirds on Lake Champlain.
Birds seen here include Horned Grebe, Common Goldeneye, Bufflehead, scoters (three species), and mergansers (three species). Large flocks of gulls congre-
gate at mid-lake to feed. Most will be Ring-billed
Gulls, but Bonaparte's Gulls may be common during
autumn. A few Great Black-backed and Herring Gulls
might be seen and the rare Little Gull sometimes
puts in a late November appearance. Return to
Lake Street and turn right. After one and one
half miles this road joins Route 17. About .75 of
a mile to the south the observer will pass the entrance to DAR State Park, which offers good seasonal
camping facilities (pay showers), picnicking and another view of the lake, providing birds similar to
those at the Tri-town Water District plant. Another
two miles down Route 17 is the Crown Point Bridge to
New York State. The small village on the Vermont
shore is known as Chimney Point. The narrows of the
lake around the bridge are excellent for migratory
waterfowl, especially during ice breakup in late
March and early April. The residences along Route
125 south of the bridge have several occupied Purple
Martin apartments on their lawns.

One mile from the junction with Route 17, Route

125 crosses Whitney Creek. A pull-out on the right
is the best stopping place for birding in this area.
Drive a half mile further and turn right into the
McCuen Slang Fishing Access. The McCuen Slang area
and the mouth of Whitney Creek are good for waders
and shorebirds especially in late summer, when there
are low water conditions along the lake. Such rarities as Little Blue Heron, Glossy Ibis, and Stilt
Sandpiper have visited here in recent years.

Just beyond the McCuen Slang Access take a left
onto the Town Line Road. This road offers more opportunities to see many of the same species seen
along the lower reaches of Jersey Street. This area
can be particularly good for Upland Sandpiper during
summer and hawks (Red-tailed, Rough-legged and American Kestrel) during the winter. A Snowy Owl is
sometimes found here in winter. The road crosses
Whitney Creek and the West and East Branches of
Dead Creek. These crossings should be checked for
waterbirds.

Upon reaching Route 22A after 4.3 miles turn
left and drive 4.1 miles north to the village of Addison. Turn left at Addison onto Route 17. One
will see the headquarters of the Dead Creek Wildlife Management Area on the right after .9 of a
mile. The fields surrounding the headquarters usually have a few Canada Geese, and there is an active
Purple Martin tenement behind the manager's resi-

Canada Geese

dence. Proceed onward for .5 of a mile and turn
right into a lot overlooking a small viewing pool
maintained for the general public. During migration
this area may harbor an interesting heron, duck, or
shorebird. Return to Route 17 and turn right proceeding west toward the creek. The fields along the
road are usually worth checking for Wild Turkey, Upland Sandpiper, Lesser Golden Plover, Horned Lark,
and Water Pipit in season. Take a left into Brilyea
Access immediately upon crossing the creek. The
marsh vegetation is at its densest here, and a check
anywhere could produce Great Blue Heron, Canada Goose
Mallard, American Black Duck, Marsh Wren, Common Yellowthroat, and Swamp Sparrow. Other species which
require more careful searching include Blue- and
Green-winged Teal, Wood Duck, Green Heron, Least Bittern (uncommon), American Bittern, Black-crowned
Night Heron, Virginia Rail, Sora (Both of these rails
are best located through the judicious use of tapes.),
and Common Gallinule. At the terminus of the road
there are two parking areas. The open water here
usually has a few Black Terns (May-August), and Ring-
billed Gulls. Other birds seen here include six
species of swallows, Belted Kingfisher, Green Heron,
Osprey, Spotted and Solitary Sandpiper (the latter in
May and July-September). The woodlots harbor Great
Horned and Common Screech Owl, Whip-poor-will, Yellow-billed and Black-billed Cuckoo, Great Crested
Flycatcher, Eastern Pewee, Red-eyed Vireo, American
Redstart, Northern Oriole, Scarlet Tanager, Northern
Cardinal, and American Goldfinch. During the warmer
months of the year, keep an eye skyward, as the Turkey Vulture is common in this area, and groups of up
to fifteen are sometimes seen lazily soaring overhead.

13. CAMEL'S HUMP

Recommended Time to Visit: May 20 - July 30

　　Camel's Hump is an imposing and distinctively
shaped 4,083 foot mountain, which is tied with Mt.

Ellen as the third highest peak in the state. The summit shares, with the considerably higher summit of Mt. Mansfield, the distinction of being above timber line; therefore, the summit area supports a delicate community of arctic and sub-arctic relict plants. A matter of greater interest for the bird-finder is the range of birdlife which may be seen from the base to the summit during the breeding season. Birds breeding regularly in the fine northern hardwood forests of the lower slopes include Ruffed Grouse, Barred Owl, Pileated Woodpecker, Yellow-bellied Sapsucker, Least Flycatcher, Eastern Pewee, White-breasted Nuthatch, Wood Thrush, Hermit Thrush, Veery, Solitary and Red-eyed Vireos, Black-and-white, Black-throated Blue, Black-throated Green, Blackburnian and Canada Warblers, Ovenbird, American Redstart, Scarlet Tanager, and Rose-breasted Grosbeak. The spruce-fir woodlands found above the 3,000 foot contour and in patches below that elevation harbor the following: Yellow-bellied Flycatcher, Red-breasted Nuthatch, Brown Creeper, Winter Wren, Swainson's Thrush, Grey-cheeked Thrush (above 3,500 feet in stunted growth), Golden-crowned Kinglet, Nashville Warbler (around brushy openings), Magnolia, Yellow-rumped and Blackpoll Warblers (Blackpoll above 3,000 feet), Purple Finch, Northern Junco, and White-throated Sparrow. Although the only bird species breeding in the krummholz and alpine vegetation on the highest altitudes appears to be the Northern Junco, the view from the summit is well worth the effort. A word of caution: please stay on the trails to avoid crushing the rare plants growing among the Bigelow's Sedge and Bilberry.

The summit of the mountain may be reached via a great number of routes; all are excellent for bird observation. Most frequently used is the Forestry Trail. This trail starts at the Couching Lion Farm (This name refers to the original French name for the mountain, Le Leon Couchant.) in Duxbury. To reach the trail head, take the left turn off Route 2, .1 of a mile west of the junction with Route 100 in Waterbury. Pass a cemetery on the left, cross the Winooski River and turn right onto a dirt road along the river, River Road. The farm land along this road is good for observing the typical birds of open, riparian situations around the state. A few pairs of Yellow-throated Vireos nest in the woodlots along the Winooski. After 3.9 miles, turn left at the tiny village of North Duxbury and proceed for 3.3 miles to Monroe State Park where the parking area for the trail is located. The Forestry Trail reaches the summit after 3.4 miles. Most of the climb is moderate, with few difficult grades making for a pleasant day-hike. Worthwhile side trails are the Dean and Alpine Trails. The Dean Trail diverges from the Forestry Trail at 1.3 miles and follows a westerly course to Wind Gap 1.7 miles south of the summit. On the way, it passes through an area of beaver activity which might contain Chimney Swift, Olive-sided Flycatcher, Ruby-crowned Kinglet, and Mourning Warbler. The Alpine Trail crosses the Forestry Trail at approximately 2.5 miles. By proceeding to the left one may reach the summit in .7 of a mile. The forest along the Alpine Trail is of the stunted type most preferred by the Grey-cheeked Thrush.

Other short access trails from the western approaches to the mountain may be reached by driving east on an unpaved road from the center of the village of Huntington Center. Bear right at .6 of a mile and left a mile further. The most direct of the two trails originating from this road is the Burrows Trail which commences at the end of the road after bearing left once more. This trail reaches the summit after a 2.9 mile climb. More roundabout is the Forest City Trail, which begins at the end of the right fork of the road. This trail climbs 2.2 miles to the Montclair Glen Lodge on the Long Trail, 1.9 miles south of the summit.

For those interested in longer hikes and a greater vertical elevation change, there are two trails ascending the mountain from the Winooski Valley. The shorter of the two is the Bamforth Ridge

Trail which reaches the summit after 5.9 miles including some rather steep going. This trail commences from the River Road on the south bank of the
river 6.6 miles west of the bridge in Waterbury and
3.2 miles east of the river crossing in Jonesville.
The Long Trail itself commences at Jonesville and
proceeds 8.9 miles to the summit via Robbins Mountain. Both Bamforth Ridge and Robbin's Mountain offer sweeping views of the Winooski Valley and have
been used by hawk watchers with modest results. For
a more detailed reference to these trails, one should
obtain a copy of the Guide Book of the Long Trail
published by the Green Mountain Club, Inc.

14. MOUNT MANSFIELD

Recommended Time to Visit: May 30 - July 15

Birding during the summer months on the highest
mountain in Vermont (4,393 feet) is often a rewarding experience. There is nothing quite like the
evening and morning choruses of Grey-cheeked and
Swainson's Thrushes. The singing may continue into
the day when clouds wrap the summit and upper slopes.
The mountain also possesses the only extensive alpine tundra in the state. The various peaks of the
ridge bear the names Nose, Chin, Adam's Apple, etc.
due to the mountain's vague resemblance to the pro-
file of a man.

Mt. Mansfield is best reached by taking state
Route 108 northwest from Stowe or south from Jeffersonville. There is a variety of methods for gaining
the upper slopes of the mountain itself. The Stowe
Corporation maintains a toll road to the ridge and
also offers gondola rides to the upper slopes. The
top station of the gondola is one hundred feet below
the summit ridge at 3,520 feet. The ridge may be
reached by using the Cliff Trail, a steep and demand-
ing trail which passes nearby to the gondola station.

The gated toll road up Mount Mansfield is found

on the left, 5.2 miles northwest of Stowe. The road ascends the mountain over a sinuous four mile course ending at the summit station complex at an elevation of 3,849 feet.

The road passes through northern hardwood forest on the lower slopes inhabited by birds typical of this widespread habitat. Above 3,000 feet conifers become prevalent with Red Spruce and Balsam Fir predominant. Birds likely to be encountered in this habitat include Yellow-bellied Flycatcher, Winter Wren, Swainson's and Grey-cheeked Thrushes, and Blackpoll Warbler. Northern Ravens may be seen or heard around the ridgeline of the mountain throughout the year.

A similar array of birds may be seen by hiking the Long Trail from Route 108. The trail head is two miles north of the base of the toll road. The trail on the west side of Route 108 ascends 1.7 miles to the Taft Lodge, a commodious (32 bunk) log building maintained by the Green Mountain Club.

Northern Ravens

There are a number of good side trails emanating from the vicinity of the lodge. These include the Profanity Trail (.5 of a mile to the ridge), and the Hell Brook and Adam's Apple Trails, .3 of a mile above the lodge, which intersect with the Bear Pond Trail on the shores of the Lake of the Clouds, a small tarn below the Adam's Apple (4,060 feet). The Long Trail proceeds steeply from this trail junction for .3 of a mile to the top of the Chin, the highest peak of the mountain. The Chin and the ridge stretching to the south nearly to the summit station are above treeline. This area closely mimics arctic tundra. Many plants are found in Vermont only here; others are shared with Camel's Hump to the south. This community of plants grows in thin, fragile soil and is easily destroyed by thoughtless hikers crushing the plants underfoot. Hikers should always walk on established trails or on rock outcroppings. The only regularly nesting birds above treeline are the Northern Junco and White-throated Sparrow. During September and October, as winter descends on the ridge, Water Pipits and Snow Buntings are seen in the alpine areas. There is a good population of Grey-cheeked Thrush around the Taft Lodge; an overnight is highly recommended.

Less heavily traveled are the trails to the summits of the mountains east of Route 108: Spruce Peak (3,320 feet), Madonna Peak (3,668 feet), and White-face Mountain (3,715 feet). These mountains have birds similar to those of Mount Mansfield and offer the added attraction of less hiker traffic. Due to the complexity of the trail system in this area, which goes well beyond the scope of this guide, the birder is directed to the Guide Book of the Long Trail published by the Green Mountain Club of Montpelier. Aside from the multitude of motels and lodges along Route 108, camping accommodations are offered at Smuggler's Notch State Park near the Mt. Mansfield and Spruce Peak Ski Areas.

Another point of interest is Bingham Falls, a

gorge on the West Branch of the Waterbury River, lined with a thick hemlock forest. This area is a mile south of the Smuggler's Notch Campground on Route 108. There is a pull-out on the east side of Route 108 with a trail which passes downhill to the falls over a quarter mile of woodland. The forest here should harbor Yellow-bellied Sapsucker, Red-breasted Nuthatch, Brown Creeper, Winter Wren, Wood and Hermit Thrushes, Solitary Vireo, Black-throated Green, Blackburnian and Canada Warblers.

Smuggler's Notch itself is a spectacular location. The notch is the high point on Route 108 between Jeffersonville and Stowe at an elevation of 2,162 feet. It is surrounded by breathtaking mountain cliffs. The most interesting bird seen here is the Northern Raven, which nests in the notch. Sometimes single birds or family groups are seen performing spectacular aerobatics within the notch.

15. BURLINGTON REGION

Season Key: Spring ***
              Summer **
              Autumn ***
              Winter **

Recommended Time to Visit: March 20 - January 30

The city of Burlington is far and away the largest municipality in Vermont. As with most urban areas, habitat for breeding and migratory birds is severely limited. However, the city offers some of the most interesting birding in Vermont.

The major influence on the "Queen City's" climate and birdlife is Lake Champlain. The lake is at its broadest here and has a significant warming effect on the climate of Burlington when it is not frozen. When frozen, the lake presents a great, reflective mantle to the sky, causing temperatures to plummet. Onshore breezes are common in the city,

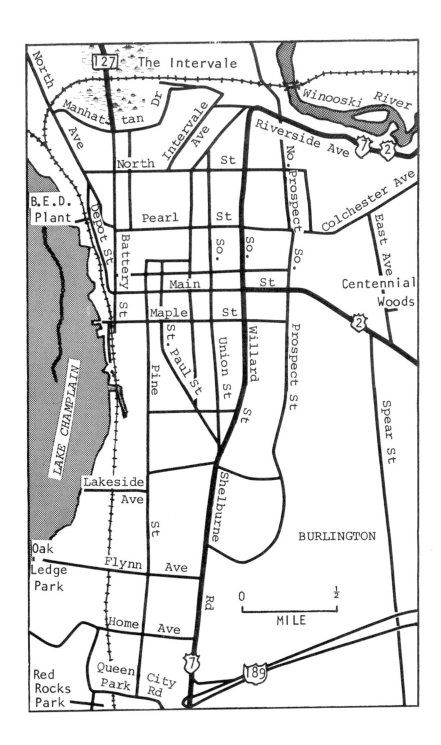

making it Vermont's "windy city". The lake also represents an important waterfowl and shorebird flyway
and, due to its north-south orientation, it also
funnels transient landbirds in their migrations to
and from Canadian breeding areas.

The observer should start explorations at the
small waterfront park at the base of Maple Street,
opposite the Lake Champlain Transport Ferry Dock.
From the park, one has a good view of the inner waters of the harbor and of the jetties which protect
the waterfront from autumn and winter storms. Birds
which frequent this area in proper season include
Mallard, American Black Duck, Common Goldeneye,
Bufflehead, Common and Red-breasted Mergansers, Great
Black-backed, Herring, Ring-billed and Bonaparte's
Gulls. Occasionally a less common bird such as a
loon or grebe, scoters, Double-crested Cormorant
(autumn), or Glaucous and Iceland Gull (November -
April) may be seen. This spot has been one of the
more reliable areas in Vermont for Snowy Owl. These
great arctic hunters may sit on lakeside buildings
or the jetty. Another good viewpoint for the waterfront is the postage stamp-sized park maintained by
the Burlington Electric Department. To reach this
location, take Battery Street and turn left onto
Depot Street. Proceed on Depot Street for about a
half mile and turn left, crossing the railroad tracks,
when the Burlington Electric Department plant is at
the left. The park is reached by going through a
gate to the lake side of the plant.

A good view of the southern portion of the harbor may be had from a promontory jutting into the
lake adjacent to the Vermont Railway Roundhouse and
the city sewage treatment plant. This location
may be reached by leaving the Maple Street waterfront
park and turning right just prior to the railroad
tracks, keeping the oil tanks on your right. Continue past the treatment facility and the roundhouse.
Bear right at the roundhouse, taking the bumpy dirt
track toward the lake. Once on the lake one should

have the outlet of the sewage treatment plant on
your immediate right. Expect the same birds seen
from the Maple Street locale. On the left, there is
a beach with two rocky islands off its shores. This
area has played host to 25 species of waterfowl and
25 species of shorebirds over the years. Large numbers of gulls roost on the rocks off the beach, including an occasional rarity (e.g. Lesser Black-
backed and Little Gulls in 1975). The best method of
viewing birds on the beach is to carefully walk down
the railroad tracks and turn onto the beach after
crossing the small bridge over a canal. Sometimes
migrant landbirds abound in the swampy woods to the
left of the tracks. Another viewpoint for this area
is the parking lot of the Blodgett's Supply Company.
This company maintains a portion of the beach as a
private park for its employees. Observers should
note that this is private property and use all due
courtesy when using this location. To reach this
spot, return to Maple Street, proceeding south to
the intersection with Pine Street. Turn right onto
Pine Street and continue for 1.25 miles and then
turn right onto Lakeside Avenue. At the end of Lakeside Avenue, Blodgett's will be directly on the
right.

Another good beach along the southern shores of
the city waterfront is at Oak Ledge Park, which may
be reached by continuing south on Pine Street and
turning right at Flynn Avenue. The park is at the
end of Flynn Avenue. Transient landbirds may be
evident in good numbers in the wooded sections of
the park in May and September when a "wave" is present.

Return to Pine Street and turn right; continue
south to Queen City Park Road and turn right. Then
turn left onto Central Avenue and take the next
right into Red Rocks Park. The park encompasses a
point jutting into the northern portion of Shelburne
Bay and includes an excellent mixed northern hardwood
forest with many good graded trails and spectacular

cliffs above the bay. This area is good for such breeding birds as Ruffed Grouse, Great Horned Owl, Pileated Woodpecker, Hairy Woodpecker, Great Crested and Least Flycatchers, Eastern Pewee, White-breasted Nuthatch, Brown Creeper, Grey Catbird, Wood Thrush, Veery, Red-eyed Vireo, Black-and-white, Black-throated Green, Blackburnian and Chestnut-sided Warblers, Northern Oriole, Scarlet Tanager, Northern Cardinal, Rose-breasted Grosbeak, and White-throated Sparrow. Transients should also be common in season with vireos, warblers, and thrushes predominating. The waters of Shelburne Bay are good for various waterbirds, and the small bay at the north end of the park has hosted such rarities as Whistling Swan, Common Eider, and Black Guillemot.

Return to Queen City Park Road and proceed straight to Shelburne Road (U.S. Route 7). Take a left and drive for about 1.3 miles to a rotary where Shelburne Road divides. Take the right branch, South Willard Street. Upon reaching Main Street, turn right, passing through the campus of the University of Vermont. Turn left onto East Avenue. Turn right onto a dirt track just beyond the University of Vermont Student Medical Center. Park here and follow the path down the hill into the extensive pine woodland below; this is Centennial Woods. This area is owned by the University of Vermont and is maintained as a natural area. Birds breeding here include Ruffed Grouse, Common Screech Owl, Great Horned Owl, Pileated Woodpecker, Great Crested Flycatcher, Eastern Pewee, Red-breasted Nuthatch, Brown Creeper, Grey Catbird, Brown Thrasher, Wood Thrush, Veery, Red-eyed Vireo, Black-and white, Yellow, Chestnut-sided and Pine Warblers, American Redstart, Eastern Meadowlark (in the fields adjacent to the woods), Scarlet Tanager, Northern Cardinal, Rose-breasted Grosbeak, Indigo Bunting, and Purple Finch. The woods is also a good place to visit during migration with good numbers of passerine migrants during spring and autumn.

71

Continue north on East Avenue, keeping an eye
and ear out for House Finch and Northern Mockingbird,
recent invaders from populations to the south. Turn
left onto Colchester Avenue, which becomes Pearl
Street, and proceed to the intersection of Pearl and
North Prospect Streets. Turn right onto North Prospect and continue to and cross Riverside Avenue.
Take Intervale Road downhill into the huge floodplain area of the Winooski River from which this
small farm road takes its name. Check the field at
left beyond the small farm at the base of the hill
during late April and early May for Cattle Egret.
This is one of the best places in the state to observe this recent colonist. One may drive out Intervale Road as far as the banks of the Winooski
River, but be forewarned that the road is usually
impassable during "mud season" in March and early
April. The Intervale floods annually, and the oxbows and ponds near the river often contain a wide
variety of dabbling ducks and an occasional shorebird. The fields along the road are good for breeding Horned Lark, Bobolink, Eastern Meadowlark, Savannah and Vesper Sparrows.

Return to Riverside Avenue and turn right.
Proceed for about .3 of a mile and turn right on Intervale Avenue. Continue to the edge of the bluff
overlooking the intervale and turn left onto Manhattan Drive. During April, the commanding view
from the bluff offers an excellent opportunity to
scan the flooded Intervale with a scope. Ducks seen
from this vantage every spring include Mallard, American Black Duck, Gadwall, American Wigeon, Common
Pintail, Northern Shoveler (about two each spring),
Blue-winged and Green-winged Teal, Wood and Ring-
necked Ducks.

An advantageous strategy is to drive or walk
down from Manhattan Drive to the Burlington Sanitary
Landfill. During late autumn, winter, and early
spring gulls of five species may be seen here. Most
frequent are Great Black-backed, Herring and Ring-

billed; however, white-winged gulls of both species occur annually in small numbers. Railroad tracks parallel the Intervale marsh and provide a fine vantage for experiencing the breeding birds of this small but productive marsh. Birds seen or heard from the tracks include American Bittern, Virginia Rail, Sora, Common Gallinule, Common Snipe, Black Tern, Marsh Wren, Common Yellowthroat, and Swamp Sparrow.

Return to Manhattan Drive and continue westward to Route 127. Turn right onto the "Beltline" which crosses the western edge of the Intervale. At the north end of the Beltline continue north on Route 127/North Avenue. A mile and a half further, take the right hand fork onto Plattsburg Avenue/Route 127. Cross the Winooski River and continue to the intersection of McCrae Road and Route 127. Turn right onto McCrae Road and proceed 1.25 miles to that road's terminus. The backwaters of the Winooski may be good here for herons and waterfowl in spring. Return to Route 127 and proceed straight. Keeping the Colchester Drive-In Theater on the left, leave Route 127 and continue straight onto the Porter's Point Road. After 1.1 miles take a left onto Airport Road. Take the second left, Windemere Way by name, which winds through a suburban neighborhood. Park at the state fishing access on the shores of

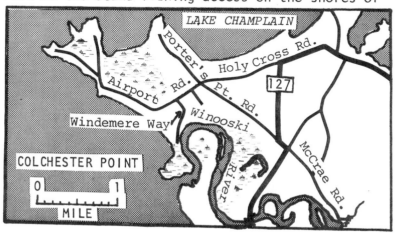

the Winooski River on the left after .6 of a mile.

Walk to the beach on the lake and scan it, the sandspit, the bay, and the marsh for various migratory waterbirds. Features at this location are waterfowl (23 species), shorebirds (23 species), herons (6 species), and gulls and terns. The time-table for the area is:

ducks after ice breakup in late March-early April, especially rafts of scaup and Canvasback

shorebirds in late May and from early August through early November; regular are Semipalmated, Black-bellied and Lesser Golden Plovers, Killdeer, Greater and Lesser Yellowlegs, Spotted Sandpiper, Common Snipe, Short-billed Dowitcher, Sanderling, Semipalmated, Least and Pectoral Sandpipers, and Dunlin

terns in August and September; up to 200 Common Terns stage here in late summer;

ducks and herons are common in September

On the left, a dirt road marks the old fill of the defunct Rutland Railroad; follow it to the river. Check the young poplar thickets for migratory landbirds in spring and autumn. The area is quite reliable for a wide variety of species, sometimes in excellent numbers. Check the flats along the mouth of the Winooski for herons, ducks, and shorebirds, especially during low water in August and September. It is often very productive to walk out the sandspit as far as is feasible; many an exciting bird has been seen at the extreme tip (e.g. Hudsonian Godwit and Red Knot).

16. SAND BAR WILDLIFE MANAGEMENT AREA AND SOUTHERN GRAND ISLE COUNTY

Season Key: Spring ***
               Summer *
               Autumn **

Recommended Time to Visit: March 20 - December 10

Northwest of Burlington lie the Champlain Islands and the delta of the Lamoille River. These areas are particularly notable for their transient waterbirds. The delta of the Lamoille (The name is a corruption of the French La Mouette, meaning gull.) supports rich swamp and marsh communities. The bays and channels of Lake Champlain around Grand Isle and North Hero sometimes host large numbers of waterfowl. This is particularly true soon after ice breakup in late March and early April.

To reach this region, proceed north from Burlington or south from St. Albans on Interstate 89 getting off at Exit 17. Proceed west from there on U.S. Route 2. After about two miles, the observer will cross the Lamoille River. About a half mile beyond the bridge one may turn left, left again, and then right, and proceed to a fishing access on the Lamoille River. One can launch a canoe or boat here and explore the river to its mouth. During late spring and summer the observer might see Green Heron, Black-crowned Night Heron, Great Blue Heron, Mallard, American Black Duck, Wood Duck, Common Goldeneye, Red-shouldered Hawk (often heard, but be cautious of Blue Jays mimicking its calls), Ring-billed Gull, and Belted Kingfisher. Sometimes the birder may be fortunate enough to see a Pileated Woodpecker flying across the river. This great bird is fairly common in the swamps and riparian woods here, and its ringing call is often heard. Birds which might be heard or seen in the floodplain forest during the warmer months are Great Crested Flycatcher, Eastern Pewee,

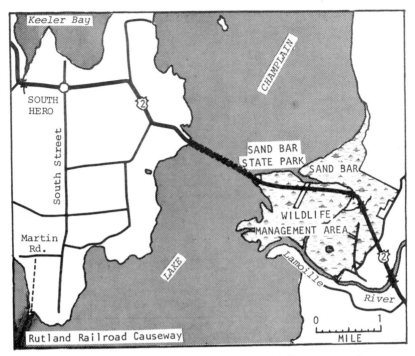

Brown Creeper, Wood Thrush, Veery, Blue-grey Gnatcatcher, Yellow-throated and Warbling Vireos, Yellow Warbler, Northern Waterthrush, American Redstart,
and Northern Oriole. There are a few pair of Cerulean Warblers breeding in this area, this being the
only known locality for this species in Vermont.
The canoeist or boater should listen carefully for
the distinctive buzzy song of this warbler. The
swamps on the right bank are owned by the State of
Vermont as waterfowl habitat. To enter this area
permission must be obtained from the Fish and Game
Department.

The observer without recourse to water craft
should continue on Route 2 west. The highway soon
becomes a causeway through the Sand Bar Silver Maple-
White Oak Swamp. As traffic is often heavy, observation from a slowly moving vehicle can be dangerous.
It is best to stop for short periods and observe
birds from the causeway on foot. Closer to the lake
the causeway borders extensive stands of Buttonbush

76

with open pools filled with emergent vegetation. A
wide variety of waterbirds may be seen from the
causeway. Some of the more common species have been
Great Blue Heron, Mallard, American Black Duck, Blue-
winged Teal, Wood Duck, Common Goldeneye, Ring-necked
Duck (April-May), and Common Snipe. Migratory shorebirds sometimes are common. Large flocks of dow-
itchers have been frequently seen during the third
week of May. At the east end of the bridge to Grand
Isle there is an unofficial boat launch on the left,
across from Sand Bar State Park. The bay here can
be excellent for migratory waterfowl and herons.

To bird Grand Isle County, one should continue
west on Route 2, proceeding across the causeway and
bridge to the township of South Hero. During late
March and early April, especially when there is a
limited area of open water under and around the
bridge, there may be a concentration of ducks. The
most frequently encountered species are Common Goldeneye and Common Merganser. The Common Tern may be
seen in small numbers in May through September.

The topography of the islands of Grand Isle
County is distinct from that of the neighboring mainland. It is characteristically flat with a few rolling hills. The bedrock is limestone and limy shale
which strongly influences the plant life of the region. White Cedar is particularly common in refor-
esting fields and along shorelines. The birdlife is
that of farmland and small woodlots. Observers
should check open fields during summer for Killdeer,
Eastern Meadowlark, Bobolink, and Savannah Sparrow.
During winter these same fields may have flocks of
Horned Lark and Snow Bunting. Unique in Vermont is
the year-round presence of the Grey Partridge, uncommon along hedgerows and in grainfields. Raptors are
sometimes present in good numbers during migration
and winter; Red-tailed Hawk, Rough-legged Hawk (uncommon in winter), Northern Harrier (April-November),
and American Kestrel are the most commonly noted
species. During winter the birder should be aware

of the opportunity to see the uncommon Northern
Shrike hunting windswept fields.

A good area to view ducks directly after ice
breakup is the old Rutland Railroad Causeway, which
used to link Colchester Point with the islands. To
reach the causeway, proceed to the village of South
Hero and turn left (south) onto a paved road at the
center of town. As the observer proceeds south, a
church should be on the right. The road then passes
through the extensive Allen Orchards. At 2.5 miles,
turn right onto Martin Road. At .3 of a mile one
crosses the old railroad right-of-way, now an overgrown dirt roadway oriented north to south. Park
and walk south toward the lake. It is three quarters
of a mile to the causeway. This area should be visited as the ice starts to break in the islands.
This may be at any time from March 15 to April 10.
When there is a sizeable opening near the causeway,
large concentrations of waterfowl occur here. The
most common ducks are Common Goldeneye and Common
Merganser. Other species that are regularly present
include Canada Goose, Snow Goose, Mallard, American
Black Duck, Common Pintail, Greater and Lesser Scaup,
Canvasback (Appreciable rafts of the preceding three
species sometimes occur.), Bufflehead, Ring-necked
Duck, Hooded and Red-breasted Mergansers. Eight
other species have been seen less frequently and in
smaller numbers.

There are several other good areas north of
South Hero. To reach these, continue on Route 2
from South Hero village. Check the waters of Keeler
Bay, east of the highway, for waterbirds during migration. Turn onto Route 314 west at the north end
of the village of Keeler Bay. At Gordon's Landing,
approximately 2.4 miles beyond Keeler Bay, a ferry
transports automobiles and passengers to New York
State. This is the only year-round ferry service on
the lake. Due to the opening maintained in winter
around the landing, a few ducks winter here, and it
is one of the first places to which migrant water-

birds return in February and March. An array of ducks and geese similar to those at the Rutland Railroad Causeway may be found at this location. About .9 of a mile north of Gordon's Landing, Route 314 turns abruptly to the east and rejoins Route 2 after 2.25 miles.

If at the point Route 314 turns east the observer continues north on the dirt road along the west shore of the island, more views may be had of the lake at left. At about 1.2 miles, two islands will be evident to the northwest of a fishing access. These are Young and Bixby Islands. Young Island belongs to the Vermont Department of Fish and Game and is an important nesting island, currently supporting a large Ring-billed Gull colony, as well as nesting Herring Gull, Black-crowned Night Heron, and Cattle Egret (a few). The best method of viewing this island is to scan through a telescope from the shore at the state fishing access. In recent years, a few Double-crested Cormorants have taken to resting at the north end of Young Island in summer. After scanning from shore, the birder may return to Route 2 by turning right and proceeding straight for 2.5 miles.

More easily accessible than the Rutland Railroad Causeway and just as good at ice breakup is the area of "The Gut", the channel of Lake Champlain between the islands of Grand Isle and North Hero. The best viewing of this area is from the bridge connecting the islands on Route 2 and from Campmeeting Point in Knight Point State Park, west of the road at the north end of the bridge. Knight Point State Park offers campsites and lean-tos between Memorial and Labor Days.

Canvasbacks

17. ST. ALBANS

Season Key: Spring ** (little known)
            Summer **
            Autumn ***

Recommended Time to Visit: March 30 - December 15
  (Dependent on ice breakup and freezeup)

        This area is still little known as a birding
locality, but with several rare sightings in recent
years the potential is unmistakable. St. Albans is
a medium size railroad town and a commercial center
for the surrounding large dairy farms. To reach
St. Albans, the best approaches are via U.S. Route 7
and Interstate 89. The best birding in the area is
to be found along the shoreline of Lake Champlain.

        Turn west onto Route 36 at the center of the
city. At three miles you will enter the village of
St. Albans Bay which is, for the most part, a seasonal community. Continue north on Route 36 for .5
of a mile. On the left is St. Albans Bay State Park
which includes a landscaped picnic area and swimming
beach. The trees of the park sometimes shelter migrants during spring and autumn; there are Warbling
Vireos during the breeding season. The main attraction is the autumn flight of shorebirds on the beach.
During the fall, the beach becomes covered with
tossed-up submergent vegetation, making it unsightly
for swimmers but a haven for weary shorebirds. Regular are Semipalmated and Black-bellied Plovers,
Killdeer, both yellowlegs, Solitary, Spotted, Semipalmated, Least and Pectoral Sandpipers, Common
Snipe, Dunlin, and Sanderling. Besides shorebirds
one will also very likely see American Black Duck,
Blue-winged and Green-winged Teal, Great Blue Heron,
Ring-billed Gull, Common Tern (nesting on bay islands, May-September), Belted Kingfisher, and Purple Martin. Walk west from the park along the causeway of Route 36. On your right will be the St. Al-

bans City Sewage Lagoon which includes a fine
swamp and cattail marsh. Check the shores and snags
for herons (Great Blue, Green and Black-crowned
Night), shorebirds and rails. Scan the open water
for Mallard, American Black Duck, both teal, Wood
Duck, Common Gallinule, and Pied-billed Grebe. Large
flocks of blackbirds gather here during migration,
including Rusty Blackbird (counts to 30).

Return to your car and drive across the bridge
over the lagoon outlet and take an immediate left
down St. Albans Point. At 1.5 miles, you will cross
a brushy marsh. Turn left into the state fishing
access and walk back to the marsh, which should harbor Virginia Rail and Sora. (A tape may be needed
here.)   The swamps of the point are inhabited during summer by both cuckoos, Great Crested Flycatcher,
Wood Thrush, Veery, Blue-grey Gnatcatcher, and Yellow-throated Vireo. However, access is limited, as
most roads on the point are private; use courtesy
and discretion if you wish to check this habitat.
Continue from the access to the tip of St. Albans
Point which is 1.3 miles onward.

Here is the state-owned Kill Kare Picnic Area,
maintained as the mainland portion of Burton Island
State Park. This spot is not well explored with re-
gard to its full potential as a birding area. A look
at a map of the point will nonetheless indicate its
potential as a migrant trap during fall migration.
The trees here are tall and well spaced and offer an
easy method of viewing migrants by allowing the observer the opportunity to chase quickly moving migrants from tree to tree. Diurnal migrants such as
swallows, Blue Jays, and blackbirds may stream over
the point in appreciable numbers during the morning
hours, and night migrants may be heard calling as
they pass over in good numbers. There is a commanding view of the bay and lake which should offer
good waterbirding in season. Burton Island itself
has shown strong indications of being an excellent
migrant trap, with recent records of White-eyed Vireo

and Worm-eating Warbler (on the same day in September, 1979). Access to the island during migration is only by rented boat or canoe.

Return to Route 36 and turn left, heading north. The large hayfields surrounding the farms here harbor nesting Killdeer, Upland Sandpiper, Eastern Meadowlark, Bobolink, Red-winged Blackbird, and Savannah Sparrow. Scan the heavens, fields, and fence posts and listen for the ethereal flight songs of the Upland Sandpipers from late April to early August. Purple Martins and Cliff Swallows nest around the farms in this area. Continue north on Route 36 looking on your left over the lake. After four miles you will see a small limestone island about 150 yards offshore; this is Popasquash Island which has a large colony of Ring-billed Gulls and a smaller number of Common Terns. Sometimes a Double-crested Cormorant or two summer around the island.

18. MISSISQUOI NATIONAL WILDLIFE REFUGE AND MUD CREEK WILDLIFE MANAGEMENT AREA

Season Key: Spring ***
             Summer **
             Autumn **

Recommended Time to Visit: March 20 - December 10
                   (dependent on freezeup and breakup)

The excellent marshlands represented by Missisquoi National Wildlife Refuge, encompassing the delta of the Missisquoi River, and Mud Creek Wildlife Management Area in Alburg lie in the extreme northwestern corner of Vermont. In recent years these areas have become, undeservingly, much neglected by birders. This seems to be due to two reasons. First, the refuge and management area are relatively remote from many of the state's birders, and, second, the popularity of Dead Creek Wildlife Management

82

Area in Addison County draws many potential observers away. With good coverage, this region should be every bit as interesting as the marshland of the southern and central Champlain Lowlands.

To reach Missisquoi National Wildlife Refuge, get off Interstate 89 at Exit 21 at Swanton. Take Route 78 west through the business district. Cross the Missisquoi River in town and continue west on Route 78. About 2.25 miles beyond the bridge the observer will see the refuge headquarters on the left. The drive should be marked by a prominent sign bearing the familiar flying goose logo of the refuge system. A good nature trail originates behind headquarters and traverses floodplain forest dominated by Silver and Red Maple. Birds breeding along the trail include Great Crested Flycatcher, Eastern Pewee, White-breasted Nuthatch, Brown Creeper, Wood Thrush, Veery, Blue-grey Gnatcatcher (rare), Yellow-throated, Red-eyed and Warbling Vireos, Yellow Warbler, Common Yellowthroat, Ameri-

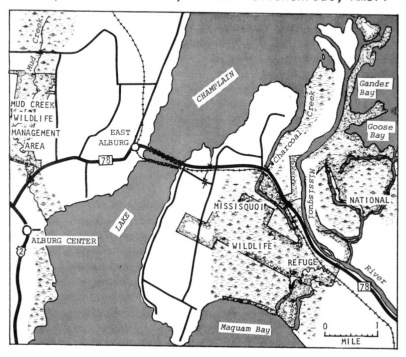

can Redstart, and Northern Oriole.

Continue west on Route 78 from headquarters.
Route 78 follows the Missisquoi for another 1.25
miles before bearing away. Sometimes ducks or
herons are seen along the river, which is often pa-
trolled by Ring-billed Gulls. A little over a mile
further the birder should park in the vicinity of
the boat ramp at Charcoal Creek. The creek is a
distributary of the Missisquoi. It is lined with
marsh vegetation backed by swamps. During migration, good numbers of waterfowl are present on the
waters of the creek. Most prevalent are Canada
Goose, Mallard, American Black Duck, Blue-winged and
Green-winged Teal, Common Pintail, American Wigeon,
Wood Duck, Ring-necked Duck, Common Goldeneye, Hooded
and Common Mergansers. Species which remain to nest
include Mallard, American Black Duck, both teal, Wood
Duck, and Common Goldeneye. Other nesting species in
the marsh and adjacent swamps are Great Blue and Green
Herons, Least (uncommon) and American Bitterns,
Northern Harrier (uncommon), Virginia Rail, Sora,
Common Gallinule, Common Snipe, Spotted Sandpiper,
Black Tern, Belted Kingfisher, Marsh Wren, and
Swamp Sparrow. A good way to explore this area,
the Missisquoi, and its other distributaries is via
boat or canoe. Of special interest to the canoeist
or boater are the wild floodplain and swamp forests
of Metcalf Island and the waters of Goose and Gander
Bays. Some of the most impressive concentrations of
waterfowl that occur within the refuge during migration are on these remote bays.

Continue west on Route 78 to the bridge to East
Alburg. Scan the lake around the bridge during migration for waterfowl, in particular bay ducks.
Loons may also be in evidence. In summer, Common
Terns often hunt over the lake. Proceed across the
bridge continuing west through the village of East
Alburg. About 1.8 miles west of East Alburg, turn
right into a state fishing access. Park and scan
the flooded timber off a little to the right for

American Black Duck, Mallard, Wood Duck, and Hooded
Merganser. Often there are herons and Osprey (April-
May and August-October) here or an occasional shorebird. On the left is the bed of the old Rutland
Railroad. The old right-of-way parallels the extensive marshes surrounding Mud Creek. A walk out the
fill is highly recommended for viewing waterfowl,
both migratory and breeding, as well as a wide variety of other nesting marsh birds. Among the species
breeding here are American and Least Bittern (rare),
Green Heron, Virginia Rail, Common Gallinule, Black
Tern, Marsh Wren, and Swamp Sparrow. Great Blue
Heron and Black-crowned Night Heron are frequent
visitors.

A nearby area with a distinctly different
habitat and birdlife is Lake Carmi State Park.
To reach the park take Route 78 east from Swanton.
At Sheldon Junction, about ten miles east of Swanton, take Route 105 east. After 4.3 miles turn left
onto the Sheldon-Franklin State Highway. The park
is on the left after about three miles. During summer, the park offers tent sites, trailer sites and
lean-tos, a naturalist program, a boat launch, and
a swimming beach. The major attraction for the
birder is the large Black Spruce-Tamarack bog at
the southwest end of the park. Birds seen here during the nesting season have included Olive-sided
Flycatcher, Boreal Chickadee (rare), Red-breasted
Nuthatch, Brown Creeper, Hermit Thrush, Veery, Golden-crowned Kinglet, Nashville, Magnolia, Yellow-
rumped and Blackburnian Warblers, Northern Waterthrush, Purple Finch, and White-throated Sparrow.
Birds breeding in the Red Maple swamp surrounding
the campsites include Great Crested and Least Flycatchers, Eastern Pewee, Wood Thrush, Red-eyed and
Warbling Vireos, and American Redstart. The lake
sometimes has summering Common Loons and should be
worthy of a check for waterfowl and divers during
migration.

19. CRAFTSBURY-GREENSBORO AREA

Season Key: Spring **
              Summer **
              Autumn ***
              Winter * (dependent on wild food)

Recommended Time to Visit: April 1 - November 30

Craftsbury and Greensboro are two of the handsomest towns in the state, replete with lakes, postcard villages, and large, hilltop dairy farms, which offer views of the surrounding mountains. Birding in this region is rewarding for the observer who chances to visit it.

A convenient place to start one's explorations of the area is the village of Greensboro, on the shores of Caspian Lake. The lake is quite large, 1.7 miles in length and, at its widest, 1.25 miles broad. Caspian Lake is an excellent place to view

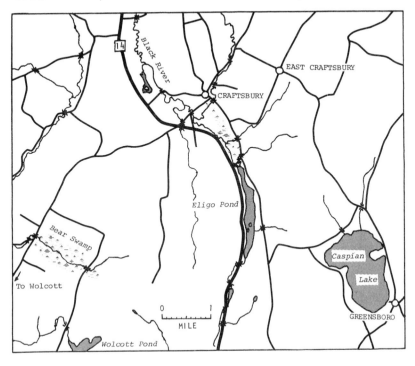

waterfowl migration, in particular in late autumn.
Common Loons are a regular feature here, sometimes
in good numbers. Other regular migrants include
Horned and Red-necked Grebes, scaup, Common Goldeneye, Bufflehead, scoters, Oldsquaw, and Common,
Red-breasted and Hooded Mergansers. The best overall
view of the lake is from the public access on the
south shore in Greensboro. A telescope is necessary
for identifying distant birds from this location.
Inquire at the Highland Inn, 1.5 miles north of the
center of town, for permission to bird from the
beach on the east shore maintained by this excellent
establishment.

Proceed north from Greensboro on the east shore
of Caspian Lake. At the north end of the lake continue straight up the hill on the paved road. This
road reaches the small village of East Craftsbury
after 6.3 miles. At the four corners in East Crafts
bury turn left and proceed down the valley of Whet-
stone Brook. At the base of this road the observer
will arrive at a paved roadway. Directly in front
of the observer are the cedar swamps in the floodplain of the Black River. During spring the floodplain west of Craftsbury is often flooded, providing
excellent waterfowl habitat. Many of the regular
transient dabbling ducks of Vermont have occurred
in the Black River Flats during spring flooding.
To the left the paved road proceeds to Route 14 and
Eligo Pond. On occasion there may be a waterbird of
interest on this long, narrow lake. To reach Crafts
bury village, turn right and proceed for about a
half of a mile. There are two left turns from the
village which cross the Black River Flats. The
first is directly after the bridge which crosses the
East Branch of the Black River. The second is a
quarter of a mile beyond the first. As well as being good for migratory dabbling ducks in spring, the
area should be good for small landbird migration in
April, May, September, and October. During summer
there are nesting Belted Kingfisher, Eastern Kingbird, Alder Flycatcher, Cedar Waxwing, Warbling

Vireo, Yellow and Chestnut-sided Warblers, Common Yellowthroat, and Swamp Sparrow. During winter there may be large flocks of American Tree Sparrows and, perhaps, a Northern Shrike. Northern Shrikes regularly winter in the Craftsbury-Greensboro area. A diligent winter search should turn one up in the river valleys or in the open country surrounding the dairy farms of the area.

Another excellent location in this area is Bear Swamp in the town of Wolcott. Bear Swamp is an extensive Black Spruce swamp along Tamarack Brook, a tributary of the Wild Branch of the Lamoille River. The swamp may be reached by taking the first left from Craftsbury across the Black River Flats. Upon reaching Route 14, cross to the unpaved road on the opposite side. Continue west on this road for 3.7 miles. At this point the road reaches Tamarack Brook. One should park at the abandoned farmhouse prior to crossing the brook. Follow the brook to the east into the swamp over blowdowns and thick coniferous growth. One may also reach the swamp by taking the first right west of the village of Wolcott on Route 15. By this route the birder will reach the Tamarack Brook crossing at three miles.

Once in the swamp, the observer should be on the alert for such birds as Wood Duck, Ruffed Grouse, Great Horned and Barred Owls, Pileated Woodpecker, Yellow-bellied and Olive-sided Flycatchers, Boreal Chickadee, Red-breasted Nuthatch, Winter Wren, Hermit and Swainson's Thrushes, Golden-crowned and Ruby-crowned Kinglets, Solitary Vireo, Tennessee (rare), Northern Parula, Magnolia, Cape May, Yellow-rumped, Black-throated Green, Blackburnian, Blackpoll, Mourning and Canada Warblers, Northern Waterthrush, Purple Finch, Northern Junco, and White-throated Sparrow. In addition to these breeding species the swamp is well worth visiting during migration. Winter finches may be abundant during winter when there is a good cone crop.

20. ST. JOHNSBURY AND ITS ENVIRONS

Season Key: Spring ***
              Summer **
              Autumn ***
              Winter *

Recommended Time to Visit: April 1 - November 30

St. Johnsbury is the commercial and transportation center for Caledonia and southern Essex Counties. The region is bounded to the east by the Connecticut River which has two large lakes, Comerford and Moore Reservoirs, created by power dams. The major watercourse of central Caledonia County is the Passumpsic River, a tributary of the Connecticut. This stream flows from the northern end of the county to Barnet. Much of this area's landscape is mountainous; the highest peak in the region is Burke Mountain, 3,267 feet in elevation. There are many fine birding areas nearby to St. Johnsbury, and some of the better ones are mentioned in this account.

The reservoirs on the Connecticut River are both very large. Comerford Reservoir is five miles long and at widest a mile broad. Moore Reservoir is even larger, nearly seven miles in length and a mile or more in width at many points along that length. During spring and autumn migrations there are often sizable concentrations of waterfowl on the surfaces of the reservoirs. During winter, the open water below the dams is attractive to wintering waterfowl, especially Common Mergansers and gulls. The reservoirs may be reached by proceeding east from St. Johnsbury on U.S. Route 2. About 2 miles east of town, turn south onto Route 18. At about 9 miles take the last right hand turn prior to crossing the Connecticut River below Moore Dam. Follow this road east for 1.2 miles. The main road bears sharply to the left at this point. The observer should proceed straight down the hill ahead to a New England

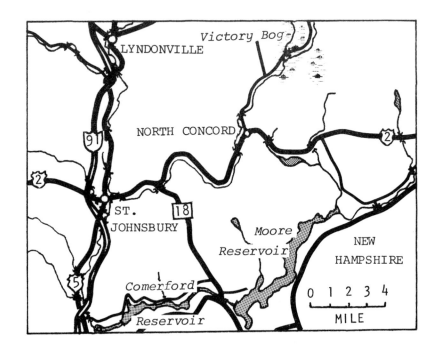

Power Company picnic area and boat launch at the
end of the road. The observer may scan the surface
of Moore Reservoir at this location. Other good
views of the reservoir may be had from the New Hampshire shoreline. These may be reached by crossing
the Connecticut River on Route 18. To reach Comerford Reservoir one should turn west off Route 18
6.8 miles south of the junction with Route 2 and
pass through the village of Lower Waterford, Vermont. This road follows a route parallel to the
reservoir. The best views of Comerford Reservoir
are from the bridge across Chandler Brook (about
2.5 miles west of Route 18) and from the dam itself which may be reached via a left hand turn off
the main road about 6.2 miles west of Route 18.
Some of the transient birds a birder might see on
these lakes are loons, grebes, Canada Goose, Mallard, American Black Duck, scaup, Ring-necked Duck,
Common Goldeneye, Bufflehead, scoters, mergansers,
and gulls. A telescope will be necessary for the
observer to allow identification of distant birds.

At any season, a visit to Victory Bog, east of
St. Johnsbury in the Moose River valley, is worthwhile for the naturalist. The area has a fine list
of breeding species of birds and is very good during migration. During years of high cone produc-
tion, it is a good location for winter finches.
The "bog" is in actuality a large collection of alder swamps, beaver ponds, and wet woodlots of
spruce and fir. From St. Johnsbury proceed east
on Route 2. At the center of North Concord, about
10.5 miles east of St. Johnsbury, turn left and
proceed north along the Moose River. The best access to the bog is via Bog Brook which lies about
6 miles north of North Concord. To explore the
bog on foot, one must be prepared to do a lot of
"creative bushwacking". A better method of exploration is to paddle Bog Brook and the Moose River
with a canoe. A partial list of breeding species
includes Great Blue Heron, American Bittern, American Black Duck, Wood Duck, Ruffed Grouse, Virginia
Rail, American Woodcock (easily located at dawn and
dusk during spring), Common Snipe, Spotted Sandpiper, Barred, Great Horned and Saw-whet Owls (the
latter is difficult to see), Ruby-throated Hummingbird, Pileated Woodpecker, Alder, Yellow-bellied,
and Olive-sided Flycatchers, Grey Jay (rare), Northern Raven, Boreal Chickadee, Red-breasted Nuthatch
Brown Creeper, Wood and Hermit Thrushes, Veery,
Golden-crowned and Ruby-crowned Kinglets, Cedar
Waxwing, Solitary Vireo, Nashville, Northern Parula
Yellow, Magnolia, Yellow-rumped, Blackburnian,
Chestnut-sided, Mourning and Canada Warblers, North·
ern Waterthrush, Rusty Blackbird (uncommon), and
Rose-breasted Grosbeak.

North of St. Johnsbury is Burke Mountain, the
second highest point in Caledonia County. The summit may be reached via automobile on a state maintained roadway. There is a day use charge for the
use of the road by motorists. To reach Burke Mountain, drive north from St. Johnsbury on U.S. Route
5 or Interstate 91 to Lyndonville, about 6.5 miles

north of St. Johnsbury. Drive through Lyndonville
on Route 5 north and turn right onto Route 114 at
the north end of town. Proceed on to the village
of East Burke about 4 miles from the junction of
Routes 5 and 114. At the north end of the village
turn right and continue east for about 2 miles.
At this point one enters Darling State Forest which
offers picnic facilities and primitive camping by
permit. The road up the mountain is steep with
many switchbacks. At the summit the birder may encounter such breeding species as Yellow-bellied
Flycatcher, Red-breasted Nuthatch, Winter Wren,
Swainson's and Grey-cheeked Thrushes (There are
about four or five pair of the latter.), Golden-
crowned Kinglet, Magnolia, Yellow-rumped, Blackpoll
and Canada Warblers, Northern Junco, and White-
throated Sparrow.

21. ISLAND POND REGION

Season Key: Spring ***
             Summer **
             Autumn **
             Winter ** (dependent on wild food and
                        snow conditions)

Recommended Time to Visit: year round

　　　Nestled in the granite mountains of the Northeast Kingdom of Vermont lies the small logging and
railroad town of Island Pond. The forests surrounding this lakeside village are boreal in character
and play host to some of the rarer and more local
breeding birds in the state. Start your tour at
the center of town, in front of the railroad station at the junction of Routes 114 and 105. Proceed
east on Route 105 out of the village for about 3.5
miles. Stop and pull off the road when the Island
Pond Municipal Airport is on your left. The brushy
areas around the runway harbor nesting American
Woodcock, Common Snipe, Whip-poor-will, Brown
Thrasher, Veery, Nashville and Chestnut-sided War-

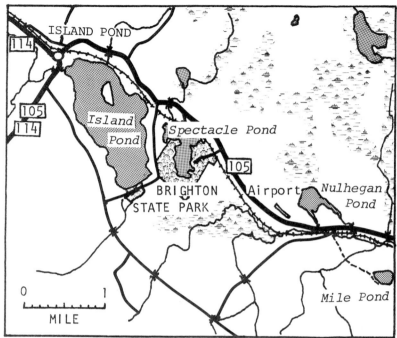

blers, Field and White-throated Sparrows. In the
early evening and just prior to dawn in spring and
early summer, one can usually hear woodcock, snipe,
and Whip-poor-will simultaneously. On the right
across the railroad tracks are the extensive alder
swamps surrounding the Nulhegan River. Nesting a-
mong the alders are American Bittern, Alder Flycatcher, Grey Catbird, Cedar Waxwing, Yellow Warbler, Northern Waterthrush, and Swamp Sparrow.
About a half mile further is the outlet of Nulhegan
Pond, where many of the species mentioned may also
be seen and heard, as well as ducks and an occasional heron. During the winter this area is usually good for Northern Goshawk and Northern Shrike.
In good years, large flocks of winter finches may
be found in the aspens and alders along the road.

Continue on for another two miles until you
arrive at a timber loading yard and railroad
crossing; this is Wenlock Crossing. Just before
the railroad crossing, there is an unpaved logging

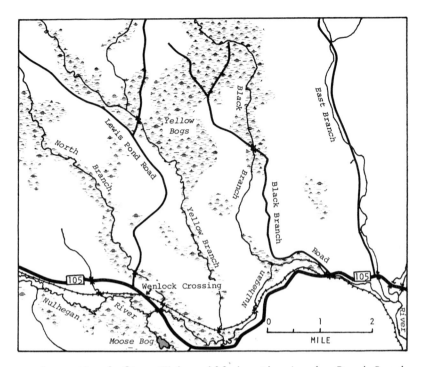

road on the left. This will be the Lewis Pond Road.
Turn onto this road and continue across the North
Branch of the Nulhegan. Exploration of the many
logging roads diverging from the main road could
offer rewards to the enterprising observer. Two
warnings must be made however. First, be careful
of truck traffic on these roads, as St. Regis log
trucks have and take the right of way here, and
you or your car could easily be flattened by a logging truck; the trucks are heavily loaded and are
nearly impossible to stop. Second, during spring
these roads can be effected very badly by the vagaries of "mud season". (St. Regis closes most roads
from late March to early May.) The area around the
North Branch can be very good for migratory warblers
in May. Nesting species include Belted Kingfisher,
Common Flicker, Eastern Kingbird, Great Crested and
Least Flycatchers, Eastern Pewee, Wood Thrush,
Black-and-white Warbler, Northern Waterthrush, Scarlet Tanager, Rose-breasted Grosbeak, and Northern
Oriole. Continuing north one will pass through

Boreal Chickadee

hardwood and coniferous forests of varying ages which harbor a wide variety of nesting birds, including sixteen species of warblers. During migration, large flocks of warblers can sometimes be found along the road.

At about five miles the road branches. The left branch is good for Black-backed Three-toed Woodpecker, Yellow-bellied Flycatcher (May to August), Northern Raven, Grey Jay, Boreal Chickadee, Red-breasted Nuthatch, and Brown Creeper. With a good cone crop winter finches may abound. The right branch continues north into the wilderness surrounding Lewis Pond. Common nesting birds along this road include Yellow-bellied Sapsucker, Winter Wren, Hermit and Swainson's Thrushes, Golden-crowned Kinglet, Solitary Vireo, Nashville, Northern Parula, Magnolia, Yellow-rumped, Black-throated Green, Blackburnian and Canada Warblers, Ovenbird, American Redstart, Rose-breasted Grosbeak, and Purple Finch. In swampy areas search for Boreal Chickadee, Olive-sided and Yellow-bellied Flycatchers, Ruby-crowned Kinglet, Philadelphia Vireo, Blackpoll Warbler, and, rarely, Tennessee Warbler.

Return to Route 105 and proceed eastward; turn right onto a logging road after about 1.5 miles. This is the South America Pond Road. Proceed from Route 105 for about a quarter of a mile until you cross a flooded cedar swamp; pull off here. Birds nesting here include Chimney Swift, Black-backed

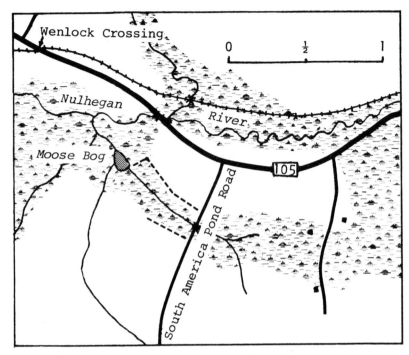

Three-toed Woodpecker (uncommon), Olive-sided Flycatcher, Tree Swallow, Grey Jay (uncommon), Boreal
Chickadee, Red-breasted Nuthatch, Brown Creeper,
Winter Wren, Hermit Thrush, Ruby-crowned and Golden-
crowned Kinglets, Nashville, Magnolia, Yellow-
rumped, Blackburnian and Canada Warblers, and Rusty
Blackbird (uncommon). Walk back toward Route 105;
turn left onto a dirt track plunging into the forest. Many of the birds already mentioned may be
seen along this road (especially Boreal Chickadee).
Also look for broods of Spruce Grouse from June
through August (rare but regular). Use care in
identifying grouse as the Ruffed Grouse is also
present. In late May and June, there may be many
Cape May Warblers singing from the tops of firs and
spruces along the road. After about a half mile
walk you will note a pond on the left. This is
Moose Bog. There is a trail down to the edge of
the mat on the left of the widening in the road.
Watch carefully for it as it is obscure.

A morning around Moose Bog can be an unforget-
table experience, with icy morning air filled with
the rich warble of the Lincoln's Sparrow from
brushy thickets, the unexpectedly loud and cheerful
song of the Ruby-crowned Kinglet, the wheezing of
Boreal Chickadees, the lisping song of the Cape May
Warbler from the spires of conifers, and the raucous
calls of a Northern Raven overhead. The bog is a
beautiful example of a heath-sedge muskeg. During
migration there is usually a waterbird of interest
here. Moose, bear, and deer may be seen here with
some luck on the part of the observer. This tract
was acquired through the Nature Conservancy by the
Vermont Department of Fish and Game.

Return to Route 105 and proceed east for about
a half mile. Take a right hand turn onto a narrow
unpaved road and drive down it for about a quarter
of a mile; park out of the way and walk along the
road. Birds that may be seen here are much the
same as in the Moose Bog area. Remember that the
Grey Jay, Black-backed Three-toed Woodpecker, and
Spruce Grouse are uncommon and unobtrusive; one
must be constantly on the lookout for them.

Return to Route 105 and continue east for three
miles; upon crossing the Nulhegan River take an immediate left turn. The unpaved road the observer
is on at this point is the Black Branch Road known
among birders as "three-toed road". The lower two
miles of this road pass through riverside hardwoods,
isolated stands of conifers, and extensive clear
cuts along the Black Branch of the Nulhegan River.
Species to be looked for are Broad-winged Hawk,
Ruffed Grouse, Spotted Sandpiper (along Black
Branch), Yellow-bellied Sapsucker, Olive-sided Fly-
catcher, Northern Raven, Red-breasted Nuthatch,
Winter Wren, Solitary Vireo, Nashville Warbler,
Northern Parula, Black-throated Blue, Yellow-rumped,
Black-throated Green, Blackburnian, Chestnut-sided,
Mourning and Canada Warblers, Northern Oriole, and
Rose-breasted Grosbeak. After about 3 miles, the

observer will cross the Black Branch and pass into the Yellow Bogs, an extensive Black Spruce forest. This area is good for Spruce and Ruffed Grouse, Black-backed Three-toed Woodpecker, Grey Jay, Swainson's Thrush, Golden-crowned and Ruby-crowned Kinglets, all of the previously mentioned warblers, plus Cape May Warbler, and Rusty Blackbird (very local along the streams).

Another worthwhile logging road may be reached from Route 105 further east. From the base of the Black Branch Road proceed east on Route 105 for another mile. Prior to the bridge over the East Branch of the Nulhegan there is a logging road on the left. It is much farther to the best habitat areas than in the case of the Lewis Pond or Black Branch Roads, but after about six miles the birder will enter an area of mixed hardwoods, clear cut, and streamside conifers. This area is good for many boreal species, including Black-backed Three-toed Woodpecker (nesting in 1980), Yellow-bellied and Olive-sided Flycatchers, Boreal Chickadee, Winter Wren, Swainson's Thrush, Solitary and Philadelphia Vireos, Mourning Warbler, and Lincoln's Sparrow.

Return to Island Pond via Route 105. Just beyond the Ethan Allen Furniture Factory is a left hand turn to Brighton State Park (marked by a small sign). The park has a naturalist program and offers camping and a fine swimming beach. A good area to check during migration is the state park beach at the south end of the park. The alders along the road often contain Wilson's Warbler during May, and Yellow Warbler, Eastern Kingbird, Brown Thrasher, and Swamp Sparrow breed here. Scan the lake during migration periods for waterbirds. Species seen here have included Common Loon, Horned and Red-necked Grebes, Double-crested Cormorant, Oldsquaw, Surf and Black Scoters, Ring-billed and Herring Gulls. Immature Common Loons often summer on the pond. Another vantage of the pond is from behind the feed store near the railroad tracks in town.

Another good area to check is Underpass Pond
in Morgan on Route 114 north of town. To reach Underpass Pond, proceed out of town on Route 114 and
continue north for 3.5 miles. Underpass Pond and
another small unnamed pond are on the right; there
are turnouts at both ponds. Birds to be seen here
include Belted Kingfisher, Yellow-bellied Flycatcher
Northern Raven, Red-breasted Nuthatch, Boreal Chickadee, Winter Wren, Hermit Thrush, Golden-crowned
and Ruby-crowned Kinglets, Solitary Vireo, twelve
species of warblers, Northern Junco, and White-
throated Sparrow.

22. NEWPORT

Season Key: Spring ***
              Summer **
              Autumn ***

Recommended Time to Visit: April 1 - December 15

This small city lies on the shores of the second largest body of water in Vermont, Lake Memphremagog. Most of the lake is in Canada, but enough
is in Vermont to allow good birding. The best approach to the city is by Interstate 91. Get off
at the southern exchange and proceed toward Newport.
Take the first right and proceed .3 of a mile to
Clyde Pond, a man-made impoundment of the Clyde
River which may harbor ducks, a Pied-billed Grebe,
or a heron. Bear left onto Upper Clyde Street and
take a right hand turn onto Riverview Street. Turn
left onto East Main Street and continue into town.
Take a right onto Union Street and an immediate
left onto Lake Street, passing through a railroad
underpass and taking an immediate right onto Park
Street. Continue straight and take the second left
onto Duchess Street, keeping North Country Union
High School on your right. Take a right on Veter-

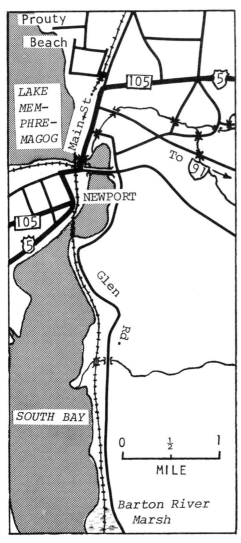

ans Avenue. On your left will be the entrance to Prouty Beach, which is maintained as a municipal park by the city of Newport. In late spring and summer there will be an attendant in the booth. (State your intentions and the attendant may pass you without charge.) During the off season, the park will be gated and you will have to walk to the beach. There is a wide view of the lake from the bluff. At Prouty Beach and at other viewpoints on the lakeshore one may see in the proper season Great Black-backed (rare), Herring, Ring-billed, and Bonaparte's Gulls, Black Tern (mid-May to August), scaup, Common Goldeneye, Bufflehead, three species of merganser, three species of scoter (October - November), Oldsquaw (October - November), Common Loon, and three species of grebe. Six species of swallow are here in the spring and summer; however, the Rough-winged Swallow is rare. Proceed to the beach on the left. There may be some shorebirds here in May, August, September, and early October. The commoner species here are Spotted Sandpiper, Killdeer, yellowlegs (both species), Least Sandpiper, Semipalmated Sandpiper, Semipalmated Plover, and Sanderling. Several other species have been seen. The shallow enclosed cove on the right seldom has anything of interest but should be checked. The thickets along its edge have good numbers of migrants under proper conditions. If nothing else, they will usually contain Yellow Warbler, Warbling Vireo, and Northern Oriole.

Return to Veterans Avenue; at its end turn right onto Freeman Street, then left on Bluff Road. Continue for a half mile and turn right onto Prouty Drive. Continue about .6 of a mile to a three-way intersection and turn left. You are now in the town of Derby. Turn left after .3 of a mile and continue north on this road through extensive hayfields above the lake. Bobolinks, Red-winged Blackbirds, and Savannah Sparrows are abundant in these fields among lesser numbers of Eastern Meadowlarks and Vesper Sparrows. After 2.8 miles you will come to a state fishing access on the left prior to a bridge crossing the John's River. Here there is a small cattail and sedge marsh, the John's River Marsh. Species found here during the breeding season include American Bittern, Virginia Rail, Sora, Common Gallinule (rare), Common Snipe, Belted Kingfisher, Willow Flycatcher, Marsh Wren, Yellow Warbler, and Swamp Sparrow. Walking the Canadian Pacific Railroad to the south a short distance gives access to Derby Bay where one might see migratory waterfowl, but remember that trains use the tracks regularly.

Return to the road and continue north. Take a left at the three-way intersection at .4 of a mile and proceed to a section of road which hugs the lake. Stop here. On your right is the Hall's Creek Marsh, which has similar birds to the John's River Marsh. On your left is a bay of the lake dotted with three islands, the largest being Black

Island. There are often loons, grebes, bay ducks, and mergansers in this bay during migration and occasionally there may be a Double-crested Cormorant. Retrace your steps to Newport, returning to Main Street. Continue down Main Street for about a quarter mile. Turn left onto Glen Road. A large body of water will now be on your right; this is South Bay. Continue onward until you see a right hand turn onto a small dirt road which crosses the railroad tracks and leads to the Newport freight yard. Stop here and scan the bay for bay ducks, loons, grebes, mergansers, and marsh ducks. There may also be Black Terns (May - August), Bonaparte's, Herring, and Ring-billed Gulls. Both Osprey and Bald Eagle are seen here occasionally. Another view of the bay may be had by continuing south on the paved road and parking in a large pull-out where you see an Agway supply depot across the tracks on the lakeshore. Continue south along Glen Road until you encounter a small fenced oil storage depot where Glen Road diverges from the railroad. Park here and walk southward on the railroad tracks through the Barton River Marsh. (It would be wise to check the freight train schedule first.) Here, during the breeding season, you may encounter American Bittern, various marsh ducks, Virginia Rail, Sora, Common Gallinule, Common Snipe, Black Tern, Willow Flycatcher, Marsh Wren, Warbling Vireo, Yellow Warbler, Common Yellowthroat, and Swamp Sparrow. Rarer sightings here have included Blue-grey Gnatcatcher (nesting in 1977), Bald Eagle, Peregrine Falcon, Least Bittern, Black-crowned Night Heron, Snowy Egret, and American Coot (probable breeding in 1980).

Return to Glen Road and retrace your route to Newport. Upon returning to Main Street, take U.S. Route 5 south. At the Coventry town line, turn left onto the Airport Road. (The turn is marked by a prominent sign.) Turn off into a small fishing access on your right just prior to crossing the Black River. The birds here are much as in the Barton

River Marsh, but you may also encounter Alder Flycatcher here. On one June night a Yellow Rail was
heard here, but there has not been a repeat record
since. Further down the road in the extensive
fields surrounding the airport, a pair of Upland
Sandpipers has bred in recent years.

23. JAY PEAK

Recommended Time to Visit: May 20 - July 30

        To reach the most northerly of the great peaks
of the Green Mountains, proceed west from Newport on
Route 105. Upon reaching the junction with Route 100
turn left on Route 100 south. At Troy, turn right
onto Route 101 north. Turn left onto State Highway 242, 3.1 miles north of Troy. Before you enter
the small village of Jay you will pass through a
small wet area. Stop, look, and listen for American Kestrel, Spotted Sandpiper, Alder Flycatcher,
Bobolink, Eastern Meadowlark, and Savannah, Vesper,
and Swamp Sparrows. Continue through Jay on Route

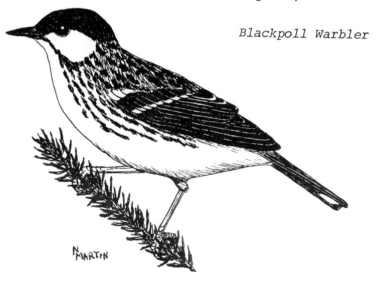

Blackpoll Warbler

242. Upon reaching the Jay Peak Ski Area access road, turn right and proceed to the base lodge. Stop along the road wherever there are brambles and saplings to listen for Mourning Warbler and Swainson's Thrush. There is a small colony of Cliff Swallows on the lodge. Be alert for Yellow-bellied Sapsucker, Olive-sided Flycatcher, and Philadelphia Vireo. Northern Ravens may be seen if one scans the sky in the direction of the mountain.

There are several ski touring trails to the north of the lodge along the tributaries of Jay Branch. There are Ruffed Grouse, Least Flycatcher, Swainson's, Wood and Hermit Thrushes, Solitary and Red-eyed Vireos, Black-throated Blue, Black-throated Green, Blackburnian and Canada Warblers, American Redstart, Scarlet Tanager, and Rose-breasted Grosbeak found here.

Returning to Route 242, follow it as it proceeds steeply to the top of the pass where the observer will find the parking space for the Long Trail. Take the trail on the north side of the road; the trail reaches the summit after 1.7 miles. The hike is a bit steep and is strenuous. The birder will encounter many of the species to be found north of the lodge during the first half mile; however, the observer will perceive subtle changes in the birdlife as one proceeds farther. The commoner species above the 3,000 foot contour are Blackpoll Warbler, Yellow-rumped Warbler, Northern Junco, and White-throated Sparrow; but the birder will also probably note Yellow-bellied Flycatcher, Brown Creeper, Winter Wren, Grey-cheeked Thrush, and Nashville Warbler. If the birder has not seen or heard these species before reaching the summit, continuing onward along the ridge toward North Jay Peak will provide more opportunities. While on the summit scan for Northern Raven, Sharp-shinned, Broad-winged and Red-tailed Hawks. With luck an observer might see Red or White-winged Crossbill, Pine Siskin, or Evening Grosbeak on this hike.

HAWKWATCHING IN VERMONT

Early in his experience, the birder becomes
acquainted with hawks, falcons, and eagles, the
diurnal raptors (as opposed to the nocturnal raptors, the enigmatic owls). The sight of a Red-
tailed Hawk perched on a dead snag, an Osprey patrolling a lakeshore, a Sharp-shinned Hawk expertly
snatching a House Sparrow from a thicket or a Merlin dashing over an open field thrills all who truly
love birds. The thrill of sighting a single individual of these superbly adapted hunters is magni-
fied many times by the experience of viewing large
numbers migrating by day. Many areas around the
world are justly famed for their raptor migrations,
involving many thousands of these birds. These
areas are blessed by qualities of location that
make them into concentration areas. Unfortunately,
such a consistently good site has yet to be dis-
covered in Vermont. However, there are many places
around the state where an observer may readily see
a hundred or more hawks on a good day. Daily watching at these sites could reward the persistent observer with a good seasonal tally.

Hawk migration observation has a long history
in Vermont. An impressive flight occurred over
Brattleboro in September of 1796. However, hawk
watching as a regular activity in the state is of
only recent origin. Prior to 1975 most hawk watching was conducted in a haphazard and highly personal
fashion by observers who were independent of each
other and rarely shared their findings. Since 1975
the Vermont Institute of Natural Science, in conjunction with the Hawk Migration Association of
North America, has collected the data of hawk watchers around the state and published them in seasonal
summaries written by dedicated, volunteer editors.
The results, while not astounding, have been inform-
ative. From 1975 to 1980, a total of 20,419 hawks
has been reported from Vermont watches during the

autumn. In this total are reports of 16 raptor species. The most common of these, as might well be expected, has been the Broad-winged Hawk with 11,192 sighted. The Sharp-shinned Hawk is solidly in second place with 2,632 reported. There have been published summaries of spring watches for three years, with a total of 3,013 hawks reported from 1979 to 1981, including 1,412 Broad-winged Hawks and 447 Sharp-shinned Hawks.

Among other things, the results have tended to indicate a lack of major concentrating features in Vermont. Hawks appear to move through the state on a broad front, selectively following local features according to weather conditions.

The fourteen most regularly reported raptors move according to separate migratory schedules, due to the various flight adaptations of each species. Broad-winged Hawks and Turkey Vultures are fairly passive soaring birds which require strong thermals to put miles behind them during migration. For this reason their migration is concentrated in the warm early autumn during the first three weeks of September. Accipiters and falcons are strong, direct fliers; they will fly in almost any weather, except during prolonged periods of precipitation. They prefer to fly with a moderate tail wind. The peak Accipiter and falcon migration in Vermont occurs from the third week of September through the second week of October. An exception to this rule is the American Kestrel; this diminutive falcon seems to use thermals extensively and is highly insectivorous. Kestrels, probably more than coincidentally, peak with the migration of dragonflies in early and mid-September. The larger Buteos, the Red-tailed, Red-shouldered and Rough-legged Hawks, and the largest Accipiter, the Northern Goshawk, have strong powered flight and move at later dates with most passing through Vermont in late October and early November. The Northern Harrier is an exception to the general rule of migratory schedules, moving throughout the season. The Osprey peaks from the first to the third week of September. There have been too few Bald Eagles reported by Vermont hawk watchers to determine a definite peak in autumn migration. Hawk flights in spring peak in April and early May.

A wide variety of locations has been used for hawk watching in Vermont over the years in most of the physiographic regions of the state. Contact the Vermont Institute of Natural Science, Woodstock, Vermont, for a current list of lookouts and official hawk watch dates. At present, however, there is no site manned in the Taconic Mountains of southwestern Vermont. Some of the more consistent locations are described below. This is in no way an attempt to limit an observer in the selection of a site; with intuition, luck, and persistence a good site may be found almost anywhere. For example, a spring count of 354 birds was made from a restaurant parking lot on Syke's Avenue in White River Junction on April 26, 1981.

The watch sites described may be handily referred to by physiographic region. They are as follows: Eastern Foothills - Putney Mountain, Putney, and Gile Mountain, Norwich. Green Mountains - Hogback Mountain and Mt. Olga, Marlboro; Robbins Mountain, Richmond; Bamforth Ridge, Bolton; Bald Mountain, Mendon (all previously mentioned in the main text; see the index); and White Rocks Mountain in Wallingford. Northeastern Highlands - Bald Mountain and Mt. Pisgah in Westmore. The Champlain Lowlands - Mt. Philo, Charlotte, and Snake Mountain in Bridport.

Directions to sites with public access are as follows:

PUTNEY MOUNTAIN Start at the general store in the village of Putney on U.S. Route 5 and proceed northwest toward Westminster West, passing the

Putney Central School on the right. Three quarters of a mile beyond the school, turn left when there is a cemetery on the right. Continue west on this road for 1.8 miles. At this intersection, cross the cross road and angle right. Proceed west on this road up Putney Mountain, bearing right at the four-cornered intersection. At 1.7 miles, prior to cresting the ridge, turn right and drive north on a relatively unimproved, dirt road. Continue north for about three quarters of a mile until the road becomes too difficult to drive; walk on from here. About a mile farther one will come to a large clearing. There is an excellent view to the north here. On many days the best hawk watching is from the steep west ridge which provides good updrafts on days with westerly winds. Some very good counts have been made here, with over 700 hawks seen on some good days.

GILE MOUNTAIN Start in Norwich at Tracy Hall (a large brick building next to the white church on Route 5). Proceed north on the Union Village Road past the general store. At .7 of a mile turn left onto Turnpike Road. At .4 of a mile, bear right. After another .6 of a mile, take the left branch and continue 4.5 miles to the end of Turnpike Road. Park by the road and take the trail on the left (indicated by both a brown and a white sign). This is a twenty minute walk of about three quarters of a mile. There is a cabin on the summit with sleeping space for four. There is a one hundred foot fire tower with a walled open top offering an unobstructed 360 degree view. Hawks generally appear from due north or over the adjoining ridge to the northwest. The best count to date has been over six hundred.

WHITE ROCKS MOUNTAIN Take Route 140 east from the village of Wallingford for 2.2 miles to a dirt road on the right. Take that road and continue past the entrance to the White Rocks National Forest Picnic Area. At 1.5 miles there is a road on

the right. Park here where the Long Trail crosses,
and follow the trail south along the road past a
house and through fields. After 1.7 miles the side
trail to White Rocks Cliff descends on the right.
The site is a cliff face which faces west overlooking the Valley of Vermont. There is no view to the
east. Hawks are seen approaching from the north
and northwest. Several counts at this locality
have exceeded 100 birds. The site is particularly
good for Accipiters and large Buteos in October.

MOUNT PISGAH   Start on Route 5A at the north
end of Lake Willoughby in the village of Westmore.
The trail to Mt. Pisgah may be taken from Route 5A
via two approaches. A trail proceeds up the mountain from the east side of 5A, 2.9 miles beyond the
junction of Routes 16 and 5A. A trail also climbs
the mountain from the south. This yellow-blazed
trail begins on an overgrown road about a half mile
south of Lake Willoughby, 5.6 miles south of the
junction of 5A and 16. After a couple hundred yards
it bears left. From the north it is 2.5 miles to
the actual summit (2,751 feet), and it is 1.7 miles
from the south. Both trails involve some steep
walking. The best hawk watching is from the north
end of the west facing cliff of the mountain which
may be reached by taking the north lookout spur
from the trail one quarter of a mile north of the
summit. Updrafts caused by westerly winds create
the best conditions for watching Accipiters, large
Buteos, and falcons which are the specialties of
this site.

BALD MOUNTAIN - WESTMORE   To reach Bald Mountain take the left off Route 5A a mile south of the
junction with Route 16. Proceed on this road for
about .6 of a mile and bear right at the fork. At
1.3 miles turn right and continue for 1.8 miles until
one perceives an unpaved road on the right. (Look
for a sign indicating "Hall Mountain Fire Tower".)
Park here and follow the roadway for .6 of a mile.
At this point turn left, crossing Bald Mountain

Brook. From here the trail proceeds southward up
the mountain, reaching the summit after 2.3 miles.
This is a long and fairly strenuous hike made complex by recent logging along the trail which ob-
scures the route. At the summit (3,315 feet), there
is a 75 foot tower which offers a fine 360 degree
view of the region. This site, in spite of high
elevation, has been quite good with counts ranging
over one hundred, frequently with an upper range
of well over two hundred.

MOUNT PHILO Mount Philo is a fairly high
(960 feet) prominence on the Lake Champlain Thrust
Fault with an excellent west facing view of the
Champlain Valley from its summit. This area may
be reached by turning east off Route 7 in Charlotte
at a sign which indicates Mt. Philo State Park.
There is a road to the summit which, when it is open
(May to October), includes a nominal day use fee.
The road is gated in April and late October; at this
time the observer must hike to the summit. The best
day to date from this lookout was September 15,
1980, when over 1,100 hawks were seen from the site.
More typical good days range over 100 birds.

SNAKE MOUNTAIN This is the highest peak along
the Champlain Thrust Fault System at 1,287 feet
above sea level. The site characteristics are similar to Mt. Philo with a good view from cliffs on
the west slope of the mountain. To reach the lookout start from Bridport on Route 22A. Drive north
from the village for 4.5 miles until you reach Will-
marth Road. Turn right onto this road and proceed
to its end. Park here and proceed on foot east
through the gate and up the slope. Bear left all
the way; if one loses one's way the birder may listen for the omnipresent vehicles of the hang glider
enthusiasts who also use the cliff; they will surely
lead the observer to the right place. The hike
takes about 45 minutes. Over 500 birds have been
seen from this site on a given day. (See map on
page 56.)

ANNOTATED LIST OF THE BIRDS OF VERMONT

This list of the 254 species of birds which are seen with some regularity in the state is derived from, and is intended to be used in conjunction with, the Vermont Daily Field Card issued by the Vermont Institute of Natural Science. The field card lists the seasonal occurrence of each species. This list is intended to provide important supplemental information on population status, habitat, and range. This will, hopefully, aid the birder in finding desired species. The species accounts also include a few references to the best localities for certain local species.

Definitions for terms of abundance are as follows:

Abundant - Easily found, about 100% chance of being detected.
Very Common - Not difficult to encounter in the proper habitat, about 90% chance of being detected.
Common - Usually seen in proper habitat, about 80% chance of being detected.
Fairly Common - Usually present in proper habitat but requires some searching, about 70% chance of being detected.
Uncommon - Difficult to find, erratic distribution in proper habitat, about 50% chance of detection.
Rare - Very difficult to find even in excellent habitat, about 20% chance of detection.
Very Rare - Usually not present except under extraordinary conditions, less than 10% chance of detection.

Refer to the map of the physiographic regions of the state, used in the introduction, when consulting this list; the names of the regions are freely used in descriptions of the ranges of birds.

COMMON LOON. Fairly common migrant on the larger bodies of water in the state. Uncommon and threatened breeder on the lakes of the Northeastern Highlands. Uncommon in early winter on Lake Champlain.
RED-THROATED LOON. Rare fall migrant on Lake Champlain, sometimes seen into early winter. Very rare on other bodies of water in autumn.
RED-NECKED GREBE. Uncommon to rare migrant on the larger bodies of water in Vermont. Rare in winter on Lake Champlain.
HORNED GREBE. Fairly common migrant and early winter visitor on Lake Champlain. Uncommon migrant elsewhere on lakes, ponds, and larger rivers.
PIED-BILLED GREBE. Uncommon migrant on slow-moving waters throughout Vermont. Rare breeder, for the most part in the Champlain Lowlands.
DOUBLE-CRESTED CORMORANT. Uncommon migrant and summer visitor on Lake Champlain. Rare in other regions on rivers, lakes, and ponds. Summer visitors are frequent around Young Island in Grand Isle County.
GREAT BLUE HERON. Common migrant in the Champlain Lowlands, fairly common migrant along rivers and pond edges in other sectors. Uncommon and local nester throughout. Easily seen at Sandbar Wildlife Management Area, Missisquoi National Wildlife Refuge, and Dead Creek Wildlife Management Area.
GREEN HERON. Fairly common breeder and migrant around streams and ponds except in the higher portions of the Green Mountains.
CATTLE EGRET. Uncommon and very local breeder on the Four Brothers Islands (Essex County, New York) and Young Island in Lake Champlain. Seen during migration in other parts of the Champlain Lowlands, espe-

111

cially the Intervale in Burlington.

GREAT EGRET. Rare visitor in spring and late summer, most are seen in the Champlain Lowlands.

SNOWY EGRET. Rare visitor in spring and late summer, records are more widespread than in the previous species.

LITTLE BLUE HERON. Very rare visitor in spring and late summer.

BLACK-CROWNED NIGHT HERON. Uncommon breeder and fairly common late summer visitor in the Champlain Lowlands. Rare late summer visitor in eastern and southwestern Vermont. Most often seen at Dead Creek Wildlife Management Area.

LEAST BITTERN. Uncommon, very local, and elusive. Found in cattail marshes in western Vermont. Most often noted at Dead Creek Wildlife Management Area and West Rutland Marsh.

AMERICAN BITTERN. Uncommon to fairly common in cattail marshes, shrub swamps, and extensive wet meadows throughout Vermont. Most common in the South Bay Marshes of Lake Memphremagog, Missisquoi National Wildlife Refuge, West Rutland Marsh, Mud Creek, and Dead Creek Wildlife Management Areas.

GLOSSY IBIS. Very rare spring and autumn visitor, most records have been from the Champlain Lowlands.

CANADA GOOSE. Common migrant on water, in grain fields, and overhead throughout Vermont. Locally abundant in the Champlain Lowlands. The largest concentrations in the state occur at Dead Creek Wildlife Management Area and Missisquoi National Wildlife Refuge. Nests in the vicinity of Dead Creek and sometimes winters in good numbers when open water on Lake Champlain permits.

BRANT. Rare migrant on Lake Champlain, occasionally found on other bodies of water.

SNOW GOOSE. Uncommon migrant on water, overhead, and in grain fields throughout Vermont. May be locally common, even abundant. The largest numbers and most consistent sightings have been from the Champlain Islands and Dead Creek Wildlife Management Area.

MALLARD. Common migrant and nester in most water habitats in all regions. Uncommon and local in winter, where there is open, fairly calm, moving water.

AMERICAN BLACK DUCK. Common migrant and fairly common breeder on rivers, lakes, ponds, and in marshes. Fairly common but local in winter where there is open water. Frequently hybridizes with the Mallard.

GADWALL. Uncommon migrant and rare breeder in the Champlain Lowlands. Rare migrant in the Connecticut Valley and very rare elsewhere.

COMMON PINTAIL. Locally common migrant in the Champlain Lowlands, uncommon to rare elsewhere. Frequents marshes, ponds, and high water pools on floodplains.

GREEN-WINGED TEAL. Common migrant and rare nester in the Champlain Lowlands. Fairly common migrant in other regions.

BLUE-WINGED TEAL. Common migrant and fairly common breeder in the Champlain Lowlands. Fairly common migrant in the Connecticut Valley, uncommon and local in central Vermont. Frequents marshes and small ponds.

AMERICAN WIGEON. Fairly common migrant in the Champlain Lowlands. Uncommon and local migrant in the Connecticut Valley, sometimes seen in suitable areas in central Vermont. Found along streams, on ponds, and in marshes.

NORTHERN SHOVELER. Rare migrant on ponds throughout Vermont. Most frequently seen in the Champlain Lowlands.

WOOD DUCK. Fairly common migrant and nester throughout the state on beaver ponds and in swamps.

REDHEAD. Rare migrant on Lake Champlain.

RING-NECKED DUCK. Fairly common migrant on ponds and broad, moving waters, most common in spring. Good locations include Herrick's Cove, Lake Bomoseen, South Bay (Newport), and Missisquoi National Wildlife Refuge.

CANVASBACK. Uncommon migrant on Lake Champlain, locally very common during freezeup and breakup. Rare migrant in the Connecticut Valley, principally in spring.

GREATER SCAUP. Uncommon, sometimes very common locally as a transient. Most are seen on Lake Champlain; however, it may be seen on any large body of water. Many stay into early winter on Lake Champlain prior to freezeup.

LESSER SCAUP. Fairly common migrant and early winter visitor on Lake Champlain, more commonly encountered on other lakes than the preceding species. Difficult to separate from the Greater Scaup in the field.

COMMON GOLDENEYE. Common to very common migrant on larger bodies of water. Uncommon nester in the northern Champlain Lowlands. Fairly common but highly localized in mid-winter around open water.

BUFFLEHEAD. Fairly common transient on Lake Champlain. Uncommon to fairly common on large bodies of water elsewhere in Vermont. Fairly common in early winter on Lake Champlain.

OLDSQUAW. Rare to uncommon migrant and early winter visitor on Lake Champlain. Rare migrant on other large bodies of water in northern Vermont.

WHITE-WINGED SCOTER. Uncommon migrant on Lake Champlain and other large bodies of water in autumn. Rare in early winter on Lake Champlain.

SURF SCOTER. Uncommon fall migrant on larger lakes and rivers. Fairly common on Lake Champlain in October. Rare in early winter on Lake Champlain.

BLACK SCOTER. Fairly common but erratic autumn transient on larger lakes and waterways. The main movement occurs later in autumn than in the preceding two species. Rare in early winter on Lake Champlain.

RUDDY DUCK. Rare to very rare migrant on ponds and lakes throughout the state.

HOODED MERGANSER. Fairly common migrant and rare breeder on broad waterways, ponds, and lakes. Rare in winter where open water persists.

COMMON MERGANSER. Common transient, rare breeder, and fairly common but local winter resident on running waters and lakes.

RED-BREASTED MERGANSER. Fairly common migrant on Lake Champlain. Uncommon transient on large bodies of water in other parts of Vermont. Rare in December and January on Lake Champlain.

TURKEY VULTURE. Wide ranging over open country throughout the state. Fairly common in the Connecticut Valley and western Vermont, less regular elsewhere.

NORTHERN GOSHAWK. Due to fluctuations in its food supplies, this bird appears in variable numbers on a year to year basis. In general, the goshawk is an uncommon nesting species in the mountains and northern portions of Vermont, with most seen in heavily wooded areas. Numbers vary most in winter. During some winters, the species is uncommon throughout the state. In others, it is uncommon in the northeast and rare elsewhere.

SHARP-SHINNED HAWK. Common migrant along ridges during daylight hours. Rare and local as a nester and winter resident. Widespread in wooded and partially wooded habitats; appears to be closely associated with coniferous forest during the breeding season.

COOPER'S HAWK. Rare breeder and winter visitor and uncommon during migration. Found in most wooded and partly wooded areas but prefers hardwoods over conifers.

RED-TAILED HAWK. Fairly common breeder throughout the state and a common transient. Fairly common in winter in the Champlain Lowlands. Uncommon in winter in other parts of Vermont. Found most often in open and semi-open country. Extensive closed canopy forest is less to its liking.

RED-SHOULDERED HAWK. Uncommon nester and fairly common migrant. The preferred habitat is hardwood forest, adjacent to beaver ponds, and swamps. Most nest in the Eastern Foothills; however, a number nest in other regions, including a few in the swamps of the Champlain Lowlands.

BROAD-WINGED HAWK. Fairly common breeder and common to locally abundant migrant. During summer, this bird is widespread in northern hardwood forest. The only part of the state where it is uncommon at this time is the Champlain Lowlands, especially in Grand Isle and Addison Counties. During migration, weather has an important effect on the numbers of this rather gregarious species seen in a given day. In fall, when the largest numbers are seen, the ideal condition is the clearing of a slow-moving low pressure system from the northwest.

ROUGH-LEGGED HAWK. Numbers of this hawk vary from year to year. Uncommon to locally common in winter in the Champlain Lowlands. It is most frequent in the lake plains of Addison County. Rare elsewhere in Vermont. Frequents open country with scattered elevated perches.

BALD EAGLE. Rare year round as a summer visitor, transient and winter visitor. Most often seen near water.

NORTHERN HARRIER. Rare breeder, locally uncommon in the Champlain Lowlands. Uncommon migrant. Very rare in winter. Prefers wet margins of ponds, hayfields, and marshes. As with other hawks, it migrates diurnally along ridges. A good location to see this bird is Dead Creek Wildlife Management Area.

OSPREY. Found throughout the state as a fairly common transient and very rare breeder. Usually seen around lakes, ponds, and rivers.

GYRFALCON. Very rare winter visitor to open areas. Most records are from northern Vermont.

PEREGRINE FALCON. Rare migrant throughout Vermont. Seen on hawk watches or hunting in open country.

MERLIN. Rare transient throughout Vermont. Seen in open country or migrating along ridges.

AMERICAN KESTREL. Fairly common nester and migrant. Uncommon in winter in western Vermont. Rare in winter in the Eastern Foothills. Frequents open country with standing dead timber for nest sites and hunting perches.

SPRUCE GROUSE. Rare permanent resident of Black Spruce-Balsam Fir forest in the extreme northeastern corner of the state. There is only a single substantiated record outside of Essex County in the last ten years. Most often seen in the vicinity of Moose Bog in Ferdinand (see Island Pond section).

RUFFED GROUSE. Fairly common, but wary, permanent resident throughout the state. Found in all manner of woodland. Prefers aspen and grey birch stands.

BOBWHITE. Rare and apparently stocked. Most are seen in fall and early winter.

RING-NECKED PHEASANT. Status similar to the preceding species. Most frequent in Bennington and Rutland Counties, adjacent to nearby New

York State populations.

GREY PARTRIDGE. Uncommon and wary, permanent resident in Grand Isle and northwestern Franklin Counties. The origin of these birds is apparently the St. Lawrence plains of Quebec.

WILD TURKEY. Fairly common, but wary, permanent resident in western Vermont north to Addison County. Uncommon and increasing in the southern Connecticut Valley. Breeds in extensive deciduous woodland. Most often seen foraging in winter fields.

VIRGINIA RAIL. Fairly common nester and transient in suitable habitat throughout the state. Habitats include very wet alder swamps, cattail lined ponds, marshes, and weed choked oxbows. Most common in the marshes of the Champlain Lowlands, the marshes surrounding Lake Memphremagog, and in the West Rutland Marsh.

SORA. Uncommon breeder and fairly common migrant of cattail marshes and sedge meadows. It is most frequently encountered in West Rutland Marsh, the marshes of the Champlain Lowlands, and the marshes around Lake Memphremagog.

COMMON GALLINULE. Uncommon breeder in cattail marshes in the Champlain Lowlands, around Lake Memphremagog, and southwestern Vermont. Rare visitor to the Connecticut Valley.

AMERICAN COOT. Uncommon migrant in the marshes of the Champlain Lowlands. Rare and erratic in the other regions of Vermont.

SEMIPALMATED PLOVER. Fairly common autumn and uncommon spring transient on the shore of Lake Champlain. Rare to uncommon on periodic mudflats in other regions.

KILLDEER. Common migrant throughout the state. Frequents golf courses and mudflats, harvested and harrowed fields. Fairly common to common nester on agricultural land.

LESSER GOLDEN PLOVER. Fairly common but very local migrant during autumn in the Champlain Lowlands. Frequently seen in the freshly harrowed fields of western Addison County. Also frequents the Lake Champlain shoreline. Very rare in other parts of Vermont.

BLACK-BELLIED PLOVER. Fairly common fall and rare spring transient, principally in the Champlain Lowlands. A few are seen at other locations around the state, such as Prouty Beach in Newport.

RUDDY TURNSTONE. Uncommon fall transient on the shores of Lake Champlain. Most often seen on the Burlington waterfront.

AMERICAN WOODCOCK. Fairly common nester and migrant throughout Vermont. It is wary and unobtrusive. Most often detected on spring evenings when courting flights take place. Habitat is varied but includes two unvarying factors, thick brushy cover and water with a muddy shoreline. Found in upland fields, alder swamps, the edges of beaver ponds, and in riverbottom swamps.

COMMON SNIPE. Fairly common transient throughout the state. Fairly common but local breeder especially in northern Vermont. Frequents marshes, bogs, alder swamps, and sedge meadows. During migration habitat may include any wet or muddy situation. Some good localities include the Intervale in Burlington and Colchester Point during migration, the West Rutland Marsh, the South Bay Marshes of Lake Memphremagog, and the swamps along the Nulhegan River during summer.

UPLAND SANDPIPER. Uncommon transient and nester in the Champlain Lowlands and northern Orleans County. Inhabits hayfields and pasture land, preferring very open areas. Good locations are Dead Creek Wildlife Management Area and, in northern Franklin County, Swanton and St. Albans.

SPOTTED SANDPIPER. Fairly common migrant and nester on lakes and

ponds and along creeks and rivers throughout Vermont.
SOLITARY SANDPIPER. Fairly common migrant on ponds, lakes, along
streams, and in flooded fields in all parts of the state.
GREATER YELLOWLEGS. Fairly common to common migrant in the Champlain
Lowlands. Uncommon in other regions. Frequents ponds, lakeshores,
streams, and flooded fields.
LESSER YELLOWLEGS. Common autumn and uncommon spring migrant in the
Champlain Lowlands, noted in lesser numbers elsewhere. This species
frequents habitats similar to the larger yellowlegs.
RED KNOT. Rare migrant on lakeshores. Most records are from Lake
Champlain.
PECTORAL SANDPIPER. Fairly common autumn and uncommon spring transient
in the Champlain Lowlands, rare in other areas. Usually seen on muddy
shores in marshes and harvested fields. Also seen along the shores of
streams, lakes, and ponds. (Sometimes appears in such atypical locations as lawns.)
WHITE-RUMPED SANDPIPER. Uncommon to rare fall transient on the shores
of Lake Champlain.
BAIRD'S SANDPIPER. Rare autumn migrant in the Champlain Lowlands,
most frequently seen along the shores of the lake. A good locality
has been the Burlington waterfront.
LEAST SANDPIPER. Common migrant in the Champlain Lowlands. Fairly
common, but local, in other parts of Vermont. It may be found along
all manner of muddy shoreline. This is the most common "peep" outside
of the Champlain Lowlands.
DUNLIN. Fairly common late autumn transient along Lake Champlain, preferring sandy flats, rare in high water years. Not often encountered
in other parts of the state.
SHORT-BILLED DOWITCHER. Fairly common, but local, transient during
May and August, with most seen in the Champlain Lowlands. Seen in
marshes and on lakeshores.
LONG-BILLED DOWITCHER. The status of this difficult to identify species is uncertain, but it is probably a rare autumn migrant. Most
records have been from the Champlain Lowlands.
STILT SANDPIPER. Very rare fall transient in the Champlain Lowlands,
prefers mudflats with emergent vegetation.
SEMIPALMATED SANDPIPER. Common transient of muddy shorelines in the
Champlain Lowlands; rare elsewhere, with the exception of Lake Mem-
phremagog where it is uncommon.
WESTERN SANDPIPER. The status of this species is clouded by the dif-
ficulty of separation from the closely related Semipalmated Sandpiper.
At present, this "peep" is considered a rare autumnal migrant in the
Champlain Lowlands.
SANDERLING. Fairly common, but local, transient on the shores of
Lakes Champlain and Memphremagog. Prefers sand beaches to muddy situations. Frequently noted at Prouty Beach in Newport and in Colchester
and Burlington.
WILSON'S PHALAROPE. A very rare, but increasingly regular, visitor to
ponds, marshes, and lakeshores. All records, at present, are confined
to northern portions of the state.
NORTHERN PHALAROPE. Rare migrant on lakes and ponds, likely to be encountered in any region of the state but most frequently seen on or
near Lake Champlain.
GLAUCOUS GULL. Rare winter visitor to Lake Champlain. Usually pushed
out by freezeup in late January, with a few seen in March and April.
The best localities for this and the following species are the Burl-

ington waterfront and the Burlington sanitary landfill.

ICELAND GULL. Rare winter visitor to Lake Champlain, less likely to be seen in early spring than the preceding species.

GREAT BLACK-BACKED GULL. Uncommon winter visitor to Lake Champlain. Most records fall between late September and mid-May. May be fairly common in the Burlington area in mid-winter. Rare along rivers and on lakes in other parts of Vermont.

HERRING GULL. Common transient, breeder, and winter visitor on Lake Champlain. Uncommon, but increasing, visitor to rivers, lakes, and ponds in all other regions of the state.

RING-BILLED GULL. Abundant breeder and migrant in the Champlain Lowlands. Lingers along the lake as long as there is open water. Common in the Missisquoi, Lamoille, and Winooski drainage basins, and around Lake Memphremagog. Less common visitor and migrant in other parts of the state.

BONAPARTE'S GULL. Fairly common transient on Lakes Champlain and Memphremagog, rare in other regions.

COMMON TERN. Common, but local, nester on the islands of northern Lake Champlain. Most often seen around St. Albans Bay in summer and at Colchester Point in autumn.

BLACK TERN. Common nester in selected marshes in the Champlain Lowlands and in the Barton River Marsh in Newport. The best locations in the Champlain Lowlands are Dead Creek Wildlife Management Area and Missisquoi National Wildlife Refuge. Very rare in other sectors of Vermont.

ROCK DOVE. Common to abundant permanent resident of urban situations and large farms throughout Vermont.

MOURNING DOVE. Common breeder and partial migrant throughout Vermont. Withdraws from high elevations and northern areas in winter. Found in agricultural habitats and suburban neighborhoods, absent from heavily wooded districts.

YELLOW-BILLED CUCKOO. Uncommon breeder and migrant in western and southeastern Vermont. Prefers brushy hillsides and riparian situations. Frequently noted around West Rutland Marsh, West Haven, and Dead Creek Wildlife Management Area.

BLACK-BILLED CUCKOO. Fairly common nester and migrant throughout Vermont. Prefers forest edge and brushy areas, but may be found around openings in deep deciduous woodland. Not found in coniferous forests. Uncommon and local in Northeastern Highlands and absent from the higher elevations of the Green Mountains.

BARN OWL. Very rare permanent resident in the Champlain Lowlands. Two nesting records are known from Charlotte and Ferrisburg.

COMMON SCREECH OWL. Fairly common, but difficult to detect due to nocturnal habits, in small groves and riparian woodlands of the Champlain Lowlands. May be more widely distributed; there are several records from other regions north to southern Orleans County.

GREAT HORNED OWL. Fairly common, but local, permanent resident throughout Vermont. Prefers riparian woods and wild montane forest. Most readily detected by its resonant hooting from December to March. Another good method of finding this bird is to check any hysterical chorus of American Crows, who mightily dislike this powerful bird.

SNOWY OWL. Rare winter visitor to open country with elevated perches. Most frequently encountered in the Champlain Lowlands.

BARRED OWL. Common permanent resident of northern hardwood forest and extensive swamps. Less common than the Great Horned Owl in the open farm country of the Champlain Lowlands. Very vocal and curious; may sometimes hoot loudly during the day and may be lured into view by a good interpretation of its distinctive calls.

LONG-EARED OWL. Highly nocturnal and little known. Apparently a rare permanent resident throughout Vermont.

SHORT-EARED OWL. This bird's status changes from year to year. Rare but sometimes locally common in winter. Roosts in shelter belts and hunts over rodent infested fields. Virtually restricted to the Champlain Lowlands, Dead Creek Wildlife Management Area has been a consistently good area for seeing this species. Very rare breeder in the Champlain Lowlands.

SAW-WHET OWL. Uncommon permanent resident in mountainous and hilly districts, frequenting thick coniferous growth. Migratory status not documented but seems more frequent in the Champlain Lowlands in winter and migratory seasons. Habitats include young White Pine stands in overgrown pastures, spruce-fir woodlands and White Cedar swamps. Not easily seen, and heard most frequently from early March to late May, with the peak of calling from March 20 - April 10.

Saw-whet
Owl

MARTIN

WHIP-POOR-WILL. By most accounts, this species has declined markedly in recent decades. This seems to be due to afforestation of the brushy hillsides it seems to prefer. Uncommon migrant and nester throughout Vermont.

COMMON NIGHTHAWK. Locally common breeder around urban centers. Common migrant along major river valleys. Towns with Common Nighthawk populations include Burlington, Rutland, White River Junction, and Barre.

CHIMNEY SWIFT. Common nester and transient throughout. Most common in urban areas because of the availability of artificial nest sites, but may be seen in wild areas around beaver ponds and other areas of standing dead timber. Huge flocks roost in mill chimneys and similar sites during migration.

RUBY-THROATED HUMMINGBIRD. Fairly common nester and transient throughout Vermont. Frequents a wide array of habitats from suburban gardens to mature northern hardwood forest and is generally not found in extensive coniferous forest. Feeds on small insects, the nectar of bright tubular flowers, and the sap flowing from fresh sapsucker workings.

BELTED KINGFISHER. Fairly common nester and transient throughout the state, found around all forms of standing and running water. Rare in winter wherever there is enough open water.

COMMON FLICKER. Common nester and transient throughout, in open habitats with dead timber. Often feeds on the ground. May utilize small breaks in woodlands, such as those formed by beavers.

PILEATED WOODPECKER. Uncommon, but widespread, in mature northern hardwood forest, floodplain forest, and even in fairly small woodlots. This bird, in spite of its size, is more often detected by its workings and ringing calls than by sightings.

RED-HEADED WOODPECKER. Uncommon and exceedingly local in the Champlain Lowlands, frequenting semi-open country and nesting in dead elms. Rare in other sections of the state. Most records are from the warmer months, but a few individuals attempt to winter.

YELLOW-BELLIED SAPSUCKER. Common breeder in central, eastern, and southwestern Vermont in mature northern hardwood forest. Common migrant throughout.

HAIRY WOODPECKER. Fairly common permanent resident in forests and woodlots throughout Vermont.

DOWNY WOODPECKER. Common permanent resident in forests and woodlots throughout the state.

NORTHERN THREE-TOED WOODPECKER. Rare permanent resident in the Northeastern Highlands in mature Black Spruce-Balsam Fir woodland. Very rare winter visitor to other parts of Vermont.

BLACK-BACKED THREE-TOED WOODPECKER. Uncommon permanent resident of spruce-fir woodland in the Northeastern Highlands. Rare permanent resident in the southern Green Mountains. Rare visitor to other parts of Vermont in winter. One of the best areas for finding this bird is Moose Bog in Ferdinand.

EASTERN KINGBIRD. Common nester and transient in open and semi-open country throughout Vermont. Standing or slow-moving water is a preferred feature of this bird's habitats.

GREAT CRESTED FLYCATCHER. Fairly common transient and nester in mature hardwood forest and riparian woodland. Found in most regions; however, it is uncommon and local in the Northeastern Highlands.

EASTERN PHOEBE. Fairly common nester and transient along pond and lake shorelines and waterways. Breeds on shelves on bridges, outbuildings, houses, and cliffs. Found in all regions.

YELLOW-BELLIED FLYCATCHER. Uncommon nester in spruce-fir forests with thick mossy floors in the Northeastern Highlands and the Green Mountains above 3,000 feet. Also seen during summer in the higher Taconics (e.g. Mt. Equinox and Dorset Peak). Uncommon and inconspicuous migrant throughout the state. Prefers brushy situations when migrating.

WILLOW FLYCATCHER. Uncommon and local nester and transient. Distributed most evenly in western Vermont and the Connecticut Valley north to Newbury. It is also known from the South Bay Marshes of Newport. Frequents open, brushy areas with scattered willows or alders interspersed with sedge or grass. Poor drainage is also an important factor in habitat selection. Only safe method of separation from the following species is through the voice, which is distinctive.

ALDER FLYCATCHER. Fairly common nester and transient. Breeds in most regions of the state, but it is very sparsely distributed in the Champlain Lowlands. Breeds and migrates in very thick, brushy swamps and overgrown hillside pastures. Prefers saturated soil conditions. Separate from the preceding species only by voice.

LEAST FLYCATCHER. Common breeder and migrant in northern hardwood forest with thick understory shrubbery and aspen or grey birch groves. Found throughout the state.

EASTERN PEWEE. Fairly common breeder and migrant in northern hardwood and riparian forest. Prefers scattered, tall, dead trees for singing and hunting perches. Found in every region of Vermont.

OLIVE-SIDED FLYCATCHER. Fairly common nester in the Northeastern Highlands, Green Mountains, and Eastern Foothills. Frequents a variety of clearing types in coniferous and mixed forest. Will inhabit beaver ponds and meadows, ski areas, clear cuts, bogs, and open boreal forest. It often perches conspicuously on tall, dead trees, where it sings (often incessantly) and from whence it sallies to hawk prey or harass unwelcome avian visitors. This species is noted as an uncommon and erratic migrant throughout the state.

HORNED LARK. Uncommon and local nester in open agricultural land with sparse vegetation in the Champlain Lowlands and northern Orleans County

(Newport, Troy, Derby, etc.). This bird of open countrysides is found throughout the state as a locally common migrant. The Horned Lark is also seen in winter in the Champlain Lowlands, where it is often common on freshly fertilized fields. This species is rare and much more erratic in winter in other parts of the state.

TREE SWALLOW. Abundant migrant over watercourses and lakes throughout Vermont. A common nester where there are suitable nest cavities available.

BANK SWALLOW. Locally abundant nester. Seen along watercourses and over lakes near to silted clay banks suitable for the nest sites of this colonial species. Common migrant, largely over water, throughout the state.

ROUGH-WINGED SWALLOW. Uncommon nester in silted clay banks and chinks or holes in stone or concrete walls along watercourses and over lakes. Generally not colonial. Uncommon during migration, never far from water.

BARN SWALLOW. Abundant nester around all manner of buildings offering nest shelves, loosely colonial. Common migrant throughout.

CLIFF SWALLOW. Fairly common, but local, colonial nester. Nest sites are usually under the eaves of houses and barns; also known to use highway bridges. Fairly common migrant, usually associating with large flocks of other swallow species. Found throughout Vermont.

PURPLE MARTIN. Common nester and transient in the Champlain Lowlands. There are also a few isolated colonies in the Newport area of northern Orleans County. Rare migrant elsewhere in the state. Nests exclusively in man-made martin houses.

GREY JAY. Uncommon permanent resident in the Northeastern Highlands, rare winter visitor to other sections of the state. Inhabits thick spruce-fir forest. Frequently seen at Moose Bog, east of Island Pond. By far the least noisy and most unobtrusive Corvid in Vermont.

Blue Jay

MARTIN

BLUE JAY. Very common permanent resident of all types of woodland in all parts of the state. In most winters there is some withdrawal from the colder portions of the Northeastern Highlands.

NORTHERN RAVEN. Uncommon permanent resident in extensively wooded districts over much of the state. Rare, but increasing, migrant and winter visitor to the Champlain Lowlands.

AMERICAN CROW. Common to very common year round inhabitant of open and semi-open country. Withdraws from the Northeastern Highlands and the higher Green Mountains in winter.

BLACK-CAPPED CHICKADEE. Abundant permanent resident of all types of forest and woodlot in Vermont.

BOREAL CHICKADEE. Uncommon, but widespread, permanent resident of Orleans and Essex County spruce-fir forests. Reliable sites include Bear Swamp in Wolcott and Moose Bog in Ferdinand. Rare visitor to other parts of Vermont during the winter.

TUFTED TITMOUSE. Uncommon, but increasing, winter visitor. Usually seen at feeding stations. An unusual feature of this species' status in Vermont is that it appears to be a rare breeder limited to the river valleys of southern Vermont. In winter there are records north to Burlington, Plainfield, and St. Johnsbury.

WHITE-BREASTED NUTHATCH. Fairly common permanent resident of deciduous forest and woodlots throughout.

RED-BREASTED NUTHATCH. Fairly common permanent resident of mixed woodlands and coniferous forest. Numbers are variable in winter, especially in the Northeastern Highlands where it may range from very common to uncommon from year to year.

BROWN CREEPER. Fairly common permanent resident in mixed woodlands and floodplain forest. Nests under bark flaps on dead trees. Difficult to see due to cryptic coloration and best detected by its high pitched calls and song.

HOUSE WREN. Fairly common nester and migrant throughout Vermont. Absent from higher elevations and extensive forest. Preferred habitats are brushy swamps, hedge rows, and woodlots. Often avails itself of artificial nest sites from bird houses to crevices under the eaves of buildings.

WINTER WREN. Fairly common, but local, nester in the Taconics, Green Mountains and Northeastern Highlands. Uncommon and local during the breeding season in the Champlain Lowlands and Eastern Foothills. Fairly common, but inconspicuous, migrant throughout. Breeds in thick, mixed, or coniferous woodland. Forages and builds its nest in standing or fallen dead timber.

CAROLINA WREN. Very rare visitor and occasional nester; in brushy thickets in southern and western Vermont at all times of year.

MARSH WREN (LONG-BILLED MARSH WREN). Common, but local, nester in the cattail marshes of western Vermont and the marshes surrounding Lake Memphremagog.

SEDGE WREN (SHORT-BILLED MARSH WREN). Rare transient and nester. Frequents wet hayfields and the drier portions of marshes. Most frequently encountered in western Vermont.

NORTHERN MOCKINGBIRD. Uncommon, but increasing, permanent resident in southern and western Vermont. Making inroads in the Northeastern Highlands in recent years. Found in suburban neighborhoods and agricultural land with thick hedgerows. Largely limited to the major river valleys.

GREY CATBIRD. Common nester and migrant throughout Vermont. Frequents brushy areas such as alder swamps, overgrown pastures, pond and forest edges, and suburban plantings.

BROWN THRASHER. Nester and transient throughout Vermont. Fairly common in western and southern Vermont, becoming more local and uncommon in northeastern and north central Vermont. Absent from higher elevations. Frequents brushy second growth, especially favoring overgrown pastures.

AMERICAN ROBIN. Abundant nester and transient. Frequents a wide variety of habitats from urban plantings and clearings in deep woodlands to sub-alpine forest. Noted in all regions. Uncommon to rare in winter, usually around fruiting shrubs.

WOOD THRUSH. Migrant and nester in all regions. Common in most of Vermont, but uncommon in the Northeastern Highlands and absent from high portions of the Green Mountains. Inhabits hardwood forest down to a few acres in extent.

HERMIT THRUSH. One of the few state birds selected largely for its vocal achievements rather than conspicuous plumage or usefulness. The Hermit Thrush is distributed largely in the Taconics, Green Mountains, Eastern Foothills, and Northeastern Highlands. In these areas it is a fairly common nester and migrant in mixed deciduous and coniferous woodlands and mature stands of conifers. The state bird is erratic and uncommon in the Champlain Lowlands as a breeder but is fairly common there as a migrant.

SWAINSON'S THRUSH. Fairly common nester in the Northeastern Highlands and above 2,000 feet in the hills and mountains of the state. Frequents coniferous and mixed woodland. Common migrant throughout Vermont in woodlands and brush.

GREY-CHEEKED THRUSH. Fairly common nester on exposed ridges with stunted Red Spruce and Balsam Fir above 3,000 feet in the Taconics, Green Mountains, and scattered outlying mountains. Uncommon and unobtrusive migrant in woodlands and brush throughout the state.

VEERY. Very common breeder and transient throughout Vermont. Inhabits wet deciduous forest with thick understory vegetation, swamps, streamside thickets, and floodplain forest.

EASTERN BLUEBIRD. Uncommon in open country with scattered high perches and suitable cavities available for nesting. Scarce in the Champlain Lowlands and the Northeastern Highlands.

BLUE-GREY GNATCATCHER. Rare, but steadily increasing, transient and nester in southern and western Vermont. Favored habitats are floodplain forest and swamps. Good areas include Herrick's Cove and West Haven.

GOLDEN-CROWNED KINGLET. Fairly common nester, migrant and winter resident. Inhabits thick stands of conifers. During the breeding season, it is local below 1,000 feet in elevation and absent from the Champlain Lowlands and all but the higher elevations of the Taconics. Migrant and winter resident throughout.

RUBY-CROWNED KINGLET. Fairly common nester in the Northeastern Highlands in stands of spruce, fir, cedar, and tamarack near standing water. Uncommon and local in the Green Mountains around ponds and bogs. Fairly common migrant throughout the state in woodlots and brush.

WATER PIPIT. Local, but fairly common, migrant throughout Vermont in harrowed and harvested fields, beaches, and alpine summits.

BOHEMIAN WAXWING. Numbers are variable for this winter visitor which is seen every year in the Champlain Lowlands, usually in small numbers. In some years this waxwing may be more widespread in Vermont. Small to medium size flocks frequent ornamental fruit plantings and unpicked orchards. Mountain Ash berries are a particularly favored food.

CEDAR WAXWING. Nester, transient and winter visitor. Very common breeder throughout in swamps, forest edge, and thickets. Gregarious and erratic in winter around fruiting shrubs and trees. Most that winter are found in the Champlain Lowlands, but the species may be encountered anywhere at that time of year.

NORTHERN SHRIKE. Regular winter visitor in variable numbers. Rare to uncommon in open country with scattered high perches. Found in every region of the state. Most reliable in central and northern Orleans County.

LOGGERHEAD SHRIKE. Rare nester and migrant in the Champlain Lowlands, frequenting open country with thick hedgerows and scattered high perches. Very rare visitor in other parts of Vermont. A decreasing species.

STARLING. Abundant permanent resident of towns, cities, and farmland throughout. Very local in heavily forested districts.

YELLOW-THROATED VIREO. Fairly common nester and migrant in floodplain forest, swamps, and isolated stands of shade trees. Generally absent above 2,000 feet and rare in the Northeastern Highlands.

SOLITARY VIREO. Fairly common transient throughout Vermont. Fairly common breeder in most regions, but it is uncommon and local in the Champlain Lowlands. Inhabits northern hardwood forest with a good admixture of coniferous growth. Seems to favor Eastern Hemlock and Red Spruce over other softwoods.

RED-EYED VIREO. Abundant nesting and migratory species throughout the state. May be found in all types of deciduous forest in the state and may utilize woodlots of very small extent.

PHILADELPHIA VIREO. This bird is a nester and transient; it is an uncommon breeder in the Green Mountains and the Northeastern Highlands. Prefers open canopy deciduous woodland and forest edge. Frequently encountered in areas of selective cutting and near wood roads. Uncommon migrant throughout Vermont in woodlands and thickets. This bird's similarity to two other Vireo species (to Warbling by appearance and to Red-eyed by voice) causes it to be overlooked often by observers. The song is very important in locating nesting pairs; it is higher pitched and slower than that of the Red-eyed Vireo and, most significantly, more repetitive. Couplets or whole phrases are repeated at least two or three times in succession.

WARBLING VIREO. Breeder and transient throughout Vermont. Fairly common except in the Northeastern Highlands where it is local. Inhabits floodplain forest, swamps, and stands of shade trees.

BLACK-AND-WHITE WARBLER. Common transient and nester throughout Vermont in young deciduous forest. Shows a strong preference for birch and aspen.

GOLDEN-WINGED WARBLER. Uncommon migrant and nester in western and southern Vermont. Frequents brushy areas including alder swamps and overgrown pastures. Absent from the Green Mountains.

BLUE-WINGED WARBLER. Rare migrant and nester in southern Vermont, occupying similar habitats to the preceding species with which it interbreeds. Expected to increase at the expense of Golden-winged populations.

TENNESSEE WARBLER. Common transient throughout the state in forest and brush. Rare nester in the Northeastern Highlands in bogs and birch or alder thickets.

ORANGE-CROWNED WARBLER. Rare autumn transient throughout Vermont in thickets and coarse herbaceous vegetation.

NASHVILLE WARBLER. Common transient and nester in overgrown pastures, stunted sub-alpine forest, and young mixed deciduous and coniferous growth. Local and uncommon in the Champlain Lowlands as a breeding species.

NORTHERN PARULA WARBLER. Breeds in the Eastern Foothills, Green Mountains, and Northeastern Highlands. Local and uncommon over much of its breeding range due to its specialized habitat requirements. Fairly common in the Northeastern Highlands. Frequents lichen festooned woodlands, usually near water. Uncommon transient throughout in forest and thickets.

YELLOW WARBLER. Common migrant and nester in riparian brush throughout Vermont. Often frequents dooryard plantings.

MAGNOLIA WARBLER. Common nester in the Green Mountains, Taconics, Eastern Foothills, and Northeastern Highlands. Breeds in young stands of conifers, including Balsam Fir, all native and introduced spruce and hemlock. Common transient in all regions in forest and brush.

CAPE MAY WARBLER. Rare breeder in the Northeastern Highlands, frequenting open stands of mature spruce and fir. Uncommon migrant in all areas, prefers conifers to deciduous growth.

BLACK-THROATED BLUE WARBLER. Common nester in southwestern, central, and eastern Vermont in northern hardwood forest, nesting in understory shrubbery. Seems to be particularly fond of Hobblebush. Uncommon and local as a nester in the Champlain Lowlands. Common migrant in deciduous woods in all regions.

YELLOW-RUMPED WARBLER. Common nester in eastern and central Vermont. Nests in two distinct habitats, sub-alpine forest and open coniferous woodlands. Uncommon and local in much of western Vermont except in the sub-alpine forest of the higher Taconics. Very common migrant in a wide variety of habitats throughout the state.

BLACK-THROATED GREEN WARBLER. Breeds throughout the state in northern hardwood forest. Favors forest with Yellow Birch, whose bark it uses to construct its nest. Common in most regions but uncommon and local in the Champlain Lowlands. Common transient in all areas.

CERULEAN WARBLER. One Vermont nesting locality is known for this species at present. About three to four pair of these treetop birds nest along the Lamoille River in Milton in tall Cottonwoods and Silver Maples. This warbler also is seen as a very rare migrant in other parts of Vermont.

BLACKBURNIAN WARBLER. Found as both a breeding species and migrant. Fairly common transient throughout Vermont in tall shade trees, both broad and needle leaved. Common nester in mature coniferous and mixed hardwood and conifer forests. Places its nest very high in conifers. Very local in the Champlain Lowlands during the breeding season.

CHESTNUT-SIDED WARBLER. Very common nester and transient in young deciduous growth throughout Vermont.

BAY-BREASTED WARBLER. Rare breeding species in spruce-fir forest of the Northeastern Highlands. Fairly common migrant throughout the state.

BLACKPOLL WARBLER. Largely confined as a breeding species to montane forest of the Green Mountains, Taconics, and some outlying mountains. It is very common in stunted growth above 3,000 feet. Also noted as an uncommon nester in open brushy coniferous forest near water in the Northeastern Highlands and above 2,500 feet in the southern Green Mountains. Fairly common migratory species in all regions.

PINE WARBLER. Uncommon and local nester and transient. Frequents tall, open stands of White Pine. Records are known from all physiographic regions, but the species is erratic in distribution at best. Most frequent in the Connecticut Valley and Champlain Lowlands.

PRAIRIE WARBLER. Uncommon nester and migrant in the southern Connecticut Valley and adjacent hill country north to Woodstock and Hartford. Favors brushy abandoned pastures with much juniper, barberry, and other low deciduous growth. Records from western Vermont indicate that a small population may exist there also.

PALM WARBLER. Uncommon migrant in early spring and late autumn in brushy and semi-open areas near water.

OVENBIRD. Very common nester and transient throughout Vermont. Inhabits mature deciduous and mixed woodlands, nesting in the leaf litter. Very inconspicuous during the autumn migration.

NORTHERN WATERTHRUSH. Fairly common nester in northern and eastern Vermont frequenting swamps, beaver ponds, bogs, slow moving streams, and pond edges. Fairly common, but often overlooked, migrant at water's edge throughout the state.

LOUISIANA WATERTHRUSH. Uncommon nester and migrant in the Eastern Foothills, the Taconics, and lower elevations of the Green Mountains. Lives along fast flowing streams with gravel bars and high cutbanks. Commonly encountered in cool, hemlock-lined ravines.

CONNECTICUT WARBLER. Very rare autumn transient in thickets and coarse herbaceous vegetation near water. There are records from all regions.

MOURNING WARBLER. Breeds in all regions of the state. Fairly common in vigorous second growth in the Northeastern Highlands and Green Mountains. One of the few redeeming qualities of clear cuts is the inevitable presence of at least one pair of these warblers in the saplings, thick briars, and sedge of these areas. Uncommon and local in the Eastern Foothills, Taconics, and Champlain Lowlands. Uncommon migrant in thick brush in all sections of the state.

COMMON YELLOWTHROAT. Abundant nester and transient throughout Vermont. Habitats include overgrown pastures, alder swamps, cattail marshes, and riparian brush.

Yellow-breasted Chat

MARTIN

YELLOW-BREASTED CHAT. Very rare spring, summer, and autumn visitor. Frequents thick brush and tangles, often not far from water.

WILSON'S WARBLER. Very rare nester in alder swamps and bog edges in the Northeastern Highlands. Fairly common, but often overlooked, transient in brushy thickets of alder, birch, and willow.

CANADA WARBLER. Breeds throughout Vermont, although it is local and

uncommon in the Champlain Lowlands. Common in other regions nesting
in brushy swamps, shrub-filled ravines and undergrowth in sub-alpine
forest. Common transient in all manner of thickets in all parts of
the state.

AMERICAN REDSTART. Very common nester and migrant throughout Vermont
in young deciduous growth and northern hardwood forest with thick understory vegetation.

HOUSE SPARROW. Very common to abundant in cities, towns, and around
dairy farms. Never far from human habitation.

BOBOLINK. Common nester and migrant in hayfields throughout Vermont.
During migration the Bobolink also frequents marshes and cornfields.

EASTERN MEADOWLARK. Fairly common, but local, nester and migrant in
and near hayfields over much of Vermont. Rare in winter in freshly
fertilized fields in the Champlain Lowlands and Connecticut Valley.

RED-WINGED BLACKBIRD. Abundant transient and breeder in cattail
marshes, shrub swamps, and hayfields. Uncommon and local in the Champlain Lowlands in winter, rare at that season elsewhere.

ORCHARD ORIOLE. Rare migrant and summer visitor. Has bred at least
twice. Found in stands of shade trees and riparian woodland.

NORTHERN ORIOLE. Common transient and breeder throughout Vermont in
tall stands of shade trees and riparian woodland.

RUSTY BLACKBIRD. Uncommon and local nester in the Northeastern Highlands and Green Mountains. Frequents pond edges and slow moving
streams surrounded by alder thickets and spruce-fir forest. Found in
all regions as an uncommon to fairly common transient in swamps, harvested fields, around ponds, and along rivers. Very rare in winter.

COMMON GRACKLE. Very common nester throughout Vermont. Never far
from water. Usually nests in loose colonies in White and Red Pine but
will use a wide variety of nest sites, including young alders, hollow-
ed out stubs and bridges. Abundant migrant frequenting farmland, marshes, and shorelines. Rare in winter at feeders and in farm feedlots.

BROWN-HEADED COWBIRD. Common nester throughout Vermont. Feeding
flocks and courting groups are encountered in open and semi-open country often near livestock. Females may turn up anywhere in search of
hosts for their young. Common migrant with Starlings and other blackbirds. Uncommon in winter around farms and feeding stations.

SCARLET TANAGER. Common nester and migrant in all parts of the state
in deciduous and mixed forest. Surprisingly difficult to see, for a
gaudy bird. More often heard than seen.

NORTHERN CARDINAL. Fairly common permanent resident in southern and
western Vermont. Found in the major stream valleys of the state. Inhabits brush near habitation. Recorded north to Greensboro and St.
Johnsbury in eastern and central Vermont.

ROSE-BREASTED GROSBEAK. Common transient and breeding species throughout the state. Frequents deciduous and mixed woodlands.

INDIGO BUNTING. Common nester and transient in all physiographic regions. Inhabits second growth at forest edges and in old pastures.

DICKCISSEL. Very rare migrant, usually seen around feeding stations
and farms in company with House Sparrows.

EVENING GROSBEAK. Very common to abundant migrant and winter visitor
to feeding stations, riparian forest, and coniferous forest. Uncommon
nester in northern hardwood and spruce-fir forest in the Green Mountains and Northeastern Highlands.

PURPLE FINCH. Fairly common nester throughout Vermont, local in the
Champlain Lowlands. Habitats include suburban plantings, forest edge,
and coniferous woods. Readily attracted to feeders. Common migrant
in a variety of wooded and brushy habitats. Variable numbers in winter, usually vacates some part of the state. Presence of large numbers

seems to depend on a healthy cone crop.

HOUSE FINCH. Locally common and increasing rapidly as a permanent
resident and perhaps as a partial migrant. Most common in suburban
neighborhoods nesting in ornamental plantings, especially conifers.
Not yet recorded from the Northeastern Highlands and still something
of a novelty in central Vermont (as of the autumn of 1981).

PINE GROSBEAK. Winter visitor in variable numbers. Ranges from common to uncommon. Seen throughout the state in some years. In many
years Pine Grosbeaks are largely limited to northern Vermont. In a
few years they may not appear outside of the Northeastern Highlands.
Feeds on maple buds, cones, and persistent fruit. Often seen on road
shoulders in search of salt and gravel.

HOARY REDPOLL. Rare winter visitor in years when the Common Redpoll
is noted in abundance. Seen in open country or at feeders with large
flocks of Common Redpolls.

COMMON REDPOLL. Erratic winter visitor throughout Vermont. Follows a
pattern of being virtually absent one year and common to abundant the
next. Occasionally absences may extend to two consecutive winters.
Appears in open country with exposed weedy growth, birch and aspen
groves, and at feeding stations.

PINE SISKIN. Common to very common winter visitor and transient in
woods of all types, particularly favors conifers. A frequent visitor
to feeders. Often patchy in distribution in winter, and may be uncommon except during migration periods. Rare and unpredictable nester in
all regions in virtually every kind of coniferous growth.

AMERICAN GOLDFINCH. Very common nester and transient in shrub swamps,
hedgerows, suburban plantings, overgrown pastures, and forest edge.
Gregarious in winter. Winter populations change each year and may
range from very common to uncommon with different population levels in
each region. Often visits feeding stations.

RED CROSSBILL. Extremely erratic visitor to coniferous forest and
small stands of conifers. Especially fond of pine. There are records from all seasons; however, most records fall within migratory
periods and winter. May be locally common at times, but this species
is, in general, rarely encountered.

WHITE-WINGED CROSSBILL. The status of this species mirrors that of
the Red Crossbill. Highly erratic in coniferous stands and forests.
Prefers Eastern Hemlock, spruce of all kinds, and Balsam Fir. Both
crossbills feed in chickadee-like manner on cones, utilizing their
uniquely adapted bill structure to extract the seeds. Most records
of this bird are from the Northeastern Highlands and Green Mountains,
but it may be encountered anywhere.

RUFOUS-SIDED TOWHEE. Nester and migrant in overgrown pastures, clear
cuts, and forest edge. Fairly common in southern Vermont becoming
less common to the north. Scarce in the Northeastern Highlands and
local in the Champlain Lowlands.

SAVANNAH SPARROW. Common nester and migrant in hayfields and other
dry tall grass habitats. It is seen in all sections of the state
and is particularly common in the Champlain Lowlands and the open
dairy farming country of Orleans County.

GRASSHOPPER SPARROW. Nester and transient in dry, short grass fields
in the Champlain Lowlands and the Connecticut Valley. More prevalent
in the Champlain Lowlands where it is uncommon, the species is rare
in the Connecticut Valley.

HENSLOW'S SPARROW. Very rare visitor to Vermont during spring, summer, and autumn. Frequents fields of sedge and tall grass with

scattered small shrubs. May occasionally nest.

VESPER SPARROW. Uncommon nester and transient throughout Vermont in dry hilltop pastures, open sparsely vegetated barrens, and dry hayfields.

NORTHERN JUNCO. Fairly common nester in coniferous and northern hardwood forest in the Taconics, Green Mountains, Eastern Foothills, and Northeastern Highlands. Very common transient in woodlands, field edges, and yards throughout Vermont. A few winter in thick riparian brush and at feeding stations. One of two species which nest regularly well above treeline on the state's mountains.

AMERICAN TREE SPARROW. Fairly common winter visitor throughout Vermont in weedy fields, brushy hedgerows, and marshes. It is a frequent visitor to feeders, sometimes in large flocks, with most visits at dawn and dusk.

CHIPPING SPARROW. Common nester and migrant throughout the state. Frequents grassy forest clearings, pasture land and suburban plantings. It is usually found near a steady supply of hair for nest lining material.

FIELD SPARROW. Fairly common nester and migrant in all regions. Inhabits overgrown pastures. A fairly quiet and unobtrusive bird, it may be easily overlooked. Rare in winter, usually in the company of American Tree Sparrows.

WHITE-CROWNED SPARROW. Fairly common transient in thick brush and suburban plantings throughout Vermont.

WHITE-THROATED SPARROW. Very common breeder and migrant over much of Vermont. Local during the nesting season in the Champlain Lowlands. It is seen in coniferous woodland, overgrown pastures, forest edge, thickets above treeline, and riparian brush. Frequents all sorts of brush during migration. Uncommon winter visitor to brush piles, plantings, and feeding stations.

FOX SPARROW. Uncommon to fairly common migrant in shrub swamps, overgrown pastures, and other thick brush.

LINCOLN'S SPARROW. Fairly common nester in the Northeastern Highlands in wet, brushy pastures, alder swamps, bogs, and around beaver swamps. Often associates with Spiraea. Uncommon nester in the southern Green Mountains in similar habitats. Fairly common, but inconspicuous, transient, only detected by diligent search of brush piles, pondside thickets, and hedgerows.

SWAMP SPARROW. Fairly common nester throughout the state in alder swamps, sedge meadows, cattail marshes, and partially filled in beaver ponds. Fairly common transient in grassy fields, thickets, brush piles, and around ponds. Rare in winter in brush near open water.

SONG SPARROW. Abundant nester and transient in almost every conceivable variety of brushy or grassy area with nearby water. Uncommon winter visitor at feeding stations and in thick vegetation near open water.

LAPLAND LONGSPUR. Uncommon migrant in harvested and freshly fertilized fields throughout Vermont. Rare to uncommon winter visitor in weedy and manure covered fields, with most recorded from the Champlain Lowlands. Often associates with Horned Larks and, less frequently, with Snow Buntings.

SNOW BUNTINGS. Common to very common transient and winter visitor throughout Vermont. Occurs in weedy and freshly fertilized fields. The largest flocks of this gregarious species are seen in the Champlain Lowlands. In some particularly harsh winters, the Snow Bunting may be almost entirely absent.

USEFUL REFERENCES

The following list is a compilation of useful references for the
birder or naturalist wishing to become more familiar with the state.

A. For problems in field identification, the best general references
presently available are:

Peterson, Roger Tory. A Field Guide to the Birds of Eastern and
Central North America, revised 1980. Boston; Houghton Mifflin

Robbins, Chandler S., Bertel Bruun, Herbert S. Zimm, and Arthur
Singer. A Guide to Field Identification: Birds of North
America. New York; Golden Press, 1966

B. For general reference on the birds of Vermont:

Spear, Robert N. The Birds of Vermont. Green Mountain Audubon
Society, Post Office Box 33, Burlington, VT 05401, 1976

The Vermont Daily Field Card. Vermont Institute of Natural Science,
Woodstock, VT 05091, 1979. A list indicating the seasonal occur-
rences of 252 species of birds from data obtained from the publication, "Records of Vermont Birds". Available from the Vermont
Institute of Natural Science for $.10 a card or $1.75 for 20 cards.

Records of Vermont Birds. A quarterly publication dealing with
the distribution, abundance, and migration of Vermont birds. Pub-
Published by the Vermont Institute of Natural Science, Woodstock,
VT 05091. 1973 to present. Subscription $5 annually.

C. For general travel information, including special topics related
to outdoor activities:

Delorme, David. The Vermont Atlas and Gazeteer. David Delorme
and Company, Post Office Box 81, Yarmouth, Maine 04096. A
special feature is the superbly detailed map work illustrating
virtually all of the roads and trails in the state.

Green Mountain Club. The Guidebook of the Long Trail, revised
1977. Green Mountain Club, Post Office Box 889, Montpelier,
VT 05602. This is a detailed account of the excellent trail
which follows the spine of the Green Mountains from the Massachusetts state line to the Canadian border.

Sadler, Ruth and Paul. Fifty Hikes in Vermont. New Hampshire
Publishing Co., P.O. Box 70, Somersworth, NH 03878, 1974. This
book describes hikes up mountains outside of the Green Mountains
as well as hikes along the Long Trail.

Appalachian Mountain Club. The AMC New England Canoeing Guide.
Appalachian Mountain Club, 5 Joy Street, Boston, MA 02108. An
excellent guide to the waterways of the state for the canoeist.

D. Finally, here are some recommendations for further study of
Vermont's natural history beyond its birdlife:

Johnson, Charles W. The Nature of Vermont: An Introduction and Guide to a New England Environment. University Press of New England, P.O. Box 979, Hanover, NH 13755, 1980. This is a good overview of the geology and the natural habitats of the state. Well worth having if one has an interest in this beautiful state.

Appalachian Mountain Club. The Mountain Flowers of New England. Appalachian Mountain Club, 5 Joy Street, Boston, MA 02108, 1964 This reference is particularly valuable for hikers.

Newcomb, Lawrence. Newcomb's Wildflower Guide. Boston and Toronto; Little, Brown and Company, 1977

Peterson Field Guide Series. Boston; Houghton Mifflin. Highly recommended, includes guides to Reptiles and Amphibians, Mammals, Animal Tracks, Insects, Butterflies, Wildflowers, Ferns, and Trees and Shrubs.

VERMONT BIRDING ORGANIZATIONS

ASCUTNEY MOUNTAIN AUDUBON SOCIETY
Post Office Box 191, Springfield, Vermont 05156

CENTRAL VERMONT AUDUBON SOCIETY
Post Office Box 1122, Montpelier, Vermont 05602

GREEN MOUNTAIN AUDUBON SOCIETY
Post Office Box 33, Burlington, Vermont 05401

NORTHEAST KINGDOM AUDUBON SOCIETY
Fairbanks Museum, St. Johnsbury, Vermont 05819

OTTER CREEK AUDUBON SOCIETY
Post Office Box 482, Middlebury, Vermont 05753

RUTLAND COUNTY AUDUBON SOCIETY
Post Office Box 367, Wallingford, Vermont 05773

SOUTHEASTERN VERMONT AUDUBON SOCIETY
c/o Albert S. Watson, RD #2, Box 180, West Brattleboro, VT 05301

VERMONT INSTITUTE OF NATURAL SCIENCE
Woodstock, Vermont 05091
VERMONT BIRD ALERT: 5 pm to 8 am weekdays, 24 hours on weekends
(802)457-2779

VERMONT BOTANICAL & BIRD CLUB
c/o Dr. Fred H. Taylor, 38 East Terrace, So. Burlington, VT 05401

INDEX